3 Book Bundle
Self-Discipline, Habits, Procrastination

The Ultimate Guide to Be More Productive and Develop Self-Discipline

Book Contents

Part 1:

Self-Discipline: A How to Guide on Overcoming Laziness and Conquering Procrastination

Part 2:

Habits: How to Implement Essential Habits to Improve Productivity, Success, and Wealth

Part 3:

Procrastination: How to Stop Procrastinating, Be More Productive, and Take Action Towards Your Goals

Dibbly Publishing

Dibbly Publishing publishes books that inspire, motivate, and teach readers. Through lessons and knowledge.

Our Book Catalog

Visit **https://dibblypublishing.com** for our full catalog, new releases, and promotions.

Follow Us on Social Media

Facebook - @dibblypublishing

Twitter - @DibblyPublish

For extra content on self-improvement and personal growth visit:

https://masterlifechallenge.com

Part 1

Self-Discipline

A How to Guide on Overcoming Laziness and Conquering Procrastination

Spence Adams

The contents of this book may not be reproduced, duplicated or transmitted without direct written permission from the author.

Under no circumstances will any legal responsibility or blame be held against the publisher for any reparation, damages, or monetary loss due to the information herein, either directly or indirectly.

Legal Notice:

This book is copyright protected. This is only for personal use. You cannot amend, distribute, sell, use, quote or paraphrase any part or the content within this book without the consent of the author.

Disclaimer Notice:

Please note the information contained within this document is for educational and entertainment purposes only. Every attempt has been made to provide accurate, up to date and reliable complete information. No warranties of any kind are expressed or implied. Readers acknowledge that the author is not engaging in the rendering of legal, financial, medical or professional advice. The content of this book has been derived from various sources. Please consult a licensed professional before attempting any techniques outlined in this book.

By reading this document, the reader agrees that under no circumstances are is the author responsible for any losses, direct or indirect, which are incurred as a result of the use of information contained within this document, including, but not limited to, —errors, omissions, or inaccuracies.

© Copyright 2017 Dibbly Publishing.
All rights reserved.

FREE 10 Steps to Increase Productivity eBook

Download Your **FREE** copy of 10 Steps to Increase Productivity eBook!

Includes Readers Newsletter

Sign up to our newsletter to receive news on new book releases, discounts, and free Kindle book promotions. All books will be available as paperback, audio, on Kindle and Kindle Unlimited unless otherwise stated. We focus on publishing books that can help people in all aspects of life on a variety of topics. Start your learning journey today!

Go to the link below!

http://dibblypublishing.com/free-10stepsproductivity-ebook

Follow Us on Social Media

https://www.facebook.com/dibblypublishing/

https://twitter.com/DibblyPublish

Contents

Introduction	1
Chapter 1 What Is Self-Discipline?	3
Chapter 2 What Is Procrastination?	7
Chapter 3 How To Develop Self-Discipline	11
MOTIVATION	12
TEMPTATION	14
REWARD	15
ROUTINE	16
HEALTHY LIVING: EXERCISE, EATING AND REST	17
GRATITUDE	20
THE ART OF DISCIPLINING YOUR MIND	22
USING AFFIRMATIONS	25
GOALS	28
ORGANIZATION AND TIME MANAGEMENT	30
COMMITMENT	33
Chapter 4 Don't Be A Perfectionist	37
Chapter 5 Creating A Support Network	41
Chapter 6 Making Things Pleasurable And Fun!	47
Conclusion	51

Introduction

Do you believe that you simply aren't strong enough to persevere towards your goals? Do you fear you lack inner strength to act? Are there negative habits you want to change but can't seem to find the way? Do you start things that are healthy, but find yourself quitting out of laziness or lack of discipline? How many times have you tried to change your habits, but end up giving up, creating a loop that tells you that you are a quitter? Do you start making plans but quit before you even start?

Each of us has a time in our lives when we desire to achieve great plans or to overcome challenges. We may endeavor to make a temporary change or to complete a project that will change our course in life, but the driving force in both of those circumstances is the ability to push through difficult feelings and to resist the desire to stop when things are hard or overwhelming.

Time and time again, the one singular set of thoughts and actions that lead to success is discipline and the ability to overcome desires to put things off. Not only is discipline necessary to set and meet goals, it's also the overall answer to an enhanced sense of wellbeing and happiness in life. Accomplished people tend to find that they are happier, more adjusted and less stressed, and when tough situations do come their way, they often easily find a way through it, as they do not avoid or hide from these challenges.

Chapter 1

What is Self-Discipline?

Self-discipline seems quite simple: set a goal and follow through with the steps to meet that goal. But of course, in any situation involving human nature, it can be a bit more complex than that! Those with self-discipline tend to meet multiple criteria of enhanced emotional intelligence, mainly meaning that they can detect and identify when they feel a feeling, like stress or sadness, and they correctly identify it, instead of being stressed but calling it another feeling. They then also know what to do with that identified emotion in a healthy way. While that also seems obvious, what tends to happen with people who have a low emotional intelligence and low self-discipline is that they may identify a feeling (stressed) but instead of the ability to distance from that stress, they instead act impulsively, by avoiding a project that increases the stress, or by giving into behaviors that numb emotions like drinking. They don't make rational decisions in the face of irrational thoughts and feelings and tend to be given to avoiding pain.

The main problem with those that lack self-discipline is that most big things we endeavor to achieve all require a level of stress and hard effort. From losing weight, to getting a raise at work or even getting that job at all, stress and effort must be applied to earn things that are difficult but worth it. Stress and accomplishment go hand in hand. Those that are discipline are also able to detect that the stress is temporary and will not last, making facing that difficulty worth it. Temporary pain for long term good outcome tends to be the default setting for those who have better discipline.

Every single person is required to make many choices every day. A person with a high level of discipline or control is the one that can choose the options that are the most advantageous to our lives in the long run, choosing those over ones that might seem more pleasurable at the time. The ability to either avoid or choose again temptation or the easier path is what leads to long-term success. Making harder choices are what meets goals and contributes to success.

Self-discipline is:

> Knowing how to identify what you want and how to achieve it
>
> Knowing how to identify what you feel or think that is a distraction to your efforts
>
> Knowing how to press on past difficult feelings, past temptations and on to the end goal of accomplishment.

Self-discipline is like a muscle or habit. The more often you engage in habits that are working towards your goals and keeping you active in disciplined behaviors, the stronger those behaviors are naturally implemented into your thinking and behavior. If you don't engage in those, they depreciate. It's been called a mental muscle, and in time becomes an actual habit of discipline.

More than anything else, discipline is the strength and capability to do things that are necessary even if you don't feel like doing them in the current moment. It's the ability to withstand temptation and manage your behavior.

Chapter 2

What is Procrastination?

We know from research that people who procrastinate are connected to higher levels of stress. They also often report feeling generally worse physically and have lower self-esteem and identity. The inability to work towards a task when it feels overwhelming means not taking care of needs like saving for retirement, calling back a job opportunity or missing out on rewards for completing things early.

We've also learned over the last 15 years that procrastination is more than simply delaying an activity. True procrastination is a combination of being able to overcome anxiety or fear of a task as well as the inability to truly gauge how much time they need to get a project done. Knowing that they will suffer as a result does not change the procrastination. While time is a portion of the problem, the main issue all goes back to emotional intelligence and managing those is the foundation of the issue.

Procrastination truly can get to everyone, even those who are typically hard workers. The human species is ardently designed to avoid pain. This is a mere function of survival! We've developed over thousands of years to seek out those behaviors that feel good, like eating and sleeping, and avoiding things that are painful. The problem in our modern society is that things that feel bad are most often temporary, and self-imposed. Pain from current life is not like the pain one might have felt as a caveman simply trying to survive, but our brains still struggle to know the difference. The number one way to avoid procrastinating is to not do it in the first place!

Procrastination is almost addictive, in that it continues to feed our brain with pleasurable avoidance and often numbing type activities, and since our brains reward pleasure, this feedback loop can be difficult to shut off. We struggle to see the overall forest for the trees as we focus on the short term positive feelings, at the sake of a lost goal to accomplish something that would bring much better positivity and reward to our lives long term.

What we've also found in research is that while everyone avoids discomfort and may engage in procrastinating, that is not the same as ongoing laziness and chronic procrastination.

Procrastination is the tendency and choice to avoid things that are not, in the simplest terms, fun. Homework, working out, completing paperwork, or tedious tasks all can be put off for something more distracting and enjoyable like social media, an app on our phone, or a night out with friends. In the moment, the avoidance of our current life situations is impulsive, and feeding the impulse also feels enjoyable.

The feedback loop starts in that very moment, with a double hit of "good" feeling by giving into an impulsive and engaging in fun behaviors. It also sets up an inability to see past the current impulse and into the future when the procrastination will cause us more stress and harm. The more we give in to the impulse to quit or avoid, the harder it is to manage this stress when we must face the task again. So, after the night out on the town, the next day we must work twice as hard to complete what we put off, but working twice as hard is twice as stressful. Right when the impulse to quit arises, we must work twice as hard to avoid that impulse, lest we start procrastination and avoidance again the next day.

Chapter 3

How to Develop Self-Discipline?

So how exactly does one break the feedback loop of avoidance? The more a person avoids, the harder it is to quit. The turning point for most people is often an avoidable and regrettable ending, like a lost job, failed assignment or lost wages. Self-discipline is the ability to look at your true desires and determining that the outcomes at the end of your goals are much worthier and more enjoyable than your current impulses and distractions, and sticking with it long enough to make it through hard situations

To figure out where to start your plan towards improving self-discipline, start by asking:

1. What is the motivation?

2. What do I think will happen when this is done?

3. What will look different when this is accomplished?

4. What needs to change?

5.	What are my weaknesses?

6.	What one thing can I start today?

Acknowledging your weaknesses is never a bad thing. If you tend to ignore things that are distractions or obvious areas where you need to improve, this will not make these go away simply with avoidance. If you are a person who is prone to binging on unhealthy food, or if checking social media becomes a much larger time waster ruining your productivity, acknowledge these weaknesses. Recognizing any area you need to improve is always the first step to creating a plan. Otherwise these will sneak up and sabotage your efforts. Self-discipline is driven by changing your habits, and truly the goal of discipline is a byproduct of the changes you make in habits, routines and daily activities.

Motivation

Most of the time, the best place to start is to figure out your motivations or ending goals, or in other terms, asking yourself "what is my why" for why you are doing this. Why are you working so hard towards a goal? What is your ending final motivation? What is your answer for "why are you doing this".

Your why and what motivates you can come from many areas, including internal and external. Your reasons can include how it might make you feel, or other's feel but also what it can bring to your life. Money, stability, and a better job may be external reasons to work hard for a new job, but often they also bring internal factors like the peace that comes from financial stability, or less stress from working as many hours.

Start by writing down a list of things that you want to accomplish at the end of your goal. So, if your goal is to complete an education, what motivates you to complete that work?

1. How will you feel?

2. What will it bring to your life?

3. What will change that is better than how your life is right now?

Define exactly what you want and then make a map of how you'll need to get there. So, if you want to complete an education and you know your motivation is to feel more stable with a better job, feel happier with more time with family and less work hours, you know you need to plan on how to finish that task.

Seeking inspiration in big and small places is one of the best ways to keep on task when you're feeling impulsive, tired or ready to quit. Shrouding yourself with reminders of what inspired you to start will help inspire you to stay on that path. Start making a list or visual that reminds you of your inspiration.

One of the best ways to make an inspirational motivator

is to answer the question "5 years from now, exactly where do I want to be, and what do I have to do to get there? Conversely, what am I doing today that will prevent me from being where I want to be in 5 years?". Keep those answers where you can see them when you feel ready to quit.

Surround yourself with pictures of what your life or goal will look like. Weight loss, financial goals, a new house, a new car etc. On top of using your own words to inspire you to stay on track, visuals of what your accomplished goal will look and feel like are also good reminders to stay the course. A night out with the friends isn't worth giving up financial security in a year.

Lack of ability to stick to your goals and losing motivation is:

1. No achievable measurable goal (which we discuss later!)

2. Lack of a routine to repeat daily or weekly to meet those goals

3. Futility that arises after consistently avoiding work towards a goal

Temptation

Even when you have established what you want and how to get there, you'll find that the impulse will still strike. The difference in those who give into procrastination impulses and those who don't, is the ability to avoid temptations and remove them before they are ever a big problem in the first place.

Begin observing, for a week, the temptations in your life that allow you to give into impulses more often. Make a note of those and remove as many as you possibly can.

Identify as many of your temptations and distractions as you can, and begin to build a structure to work against them.

If your work is online or on your computer, seek out applications or web browser extensions that will turn off your access to the internet or reward you by staying on one page for a certain amount of time.

You can also shut off access to certain websites like social media. Some find a work/reward balance like shutting off social media for increments of an hour and then allowing it to be reopened for 10 minutes.

Remove any temptations like food, unhealthy activities, and build in positive rewards. Most of us do well when we are able to be rewarded when we perceive we are sacrificing something like comfort, enjoyable food or time spent doing something fun.

Reward

Make a list of things that you enjoy, even rewards that have nothing to do with your project or goal. For example, even if you are eating healthy, you can add in a reward that for every hour of studying you can have a small treat. Portion out those treats so that you also mitigate any temptation to binge.

Create a list of small and big rewards that match your goals and tasks you've created in the plan. Our next step is to discuss routine, and you can add in rewards to match your routine. Since we are motivated by pleasure, it makes sense to allow our system to continue finding pleasure, but only when a certain set of activities are accomplished, and only with healthy rewards. This helps us rewire how we see sacrifice, reward and fun, by seeing it within healthy boundaries and because of hard work, instead of a way to distract from hard work with unhealthy, impulsive behaviors.

Routine

The good part about being driven by good and positive emotions is that we can also use that to overcome procrastination. Humans also really like predictability and anything that allows us to predict what happens next feels safe and calming. Routines are one great way to allow us to reduce stress but also increase the pleasure principles that often drive procrastination. If we know that positive feelings drive our emotions, then we need to remember this value and create a predictable, stress reducing and enjoyable routine that allows us to stick to our plans, not get confused about what happens next, and feels positive as well as soothing.

Look at your motivation list for ways to create routines. If your motivations to complete an education, for example, are to feel secure financially and have a good job, then begin seeing your education as a job. A job usually has a set routine of start times, ending times, and daily tasks. If you structure your education the same way, when studying, then you are already acting as if you are working towards the job you desire. Set a start time, end time and daily study tasks as motivation to complete the work of studying. You can use what you enjoy and want to accomplish to structure the work you need to do to get you there.

Don't forget to add your rewards to your system. If your plan for routine is to study daily, and on a smaller scale, the routine is to study in small 15 minute bursts, followed by 5 minutes of social media time, then you've implemented a routine for making sure the task is accomplished by also adding in small rewards to continue.

Healthy Living: Exercise, Eating and Rest

Even if your actual goal isn't about health and wellness, eating right and exercising have multiple benefits to reducing procrastination and increasing your ability to be disciplined. People who take their goals seriously are also dedicated to pushing through things that may not be enjoyable in the moment for the positive ending benefit, like completing a hard workout because it is good for the body, or eating foods that are good for your body that may not taste as good as candy.

People who tend to be able to stick to goals do so in many areas of their life, not just one. Since the major components of discipline involve pushing through discomfort, then applying that skill to health, work and relationships is natural. The ability to stick to what you want to accomplish even when the current moment isn't enjoyable means being willing to stick to a healthy routine of eating and working out.

Study after study has produced results that show that participants who regularly exercise report decreased stress as well as overall changes to their life like decreasing smoking and drinking and increasing healthy eating. Exercise, more than any other positive behavior, continues to show that participants stick to other life plans and goals, feel more in control of their emotions and most importantly to this discussion, tend to stick to goals and commitments and feel a sense of increased motivation and change in their lives.

One change in your life can ripple into other areas of your life. A commitment to exercise seems to have the largest impact in ability to persevere to a goal. It increases fitness and mental abilities, improves mood and impulse control, reduces weight, and reduces chances to get sick.

Because of sticking to an exercise plan it also increases our ability to commit and stick to it.

It's always advisable to pick something you love to do and stick to doing that activity. If you hate running, don't run! If you love to dance, find a dance class! Exercise and goal setting never must look like anyone else's type of fitness, and everyone can move and feel better. If you've avoided it because you don't enjoy at treadmill or lifting weights, start with any kind of movement that will motivate you and keep you going.

Eating for good energy is what creates a longer lasting energy source and is good for the brain. Protein fuels the brain and body and helps to avoid energy crashes and hormone fluctuations because of carbohydrates. Leafy greens, healthy proteins and lots of water are healthy sources of energy for your brain and body.

Outside of positive health benefits, engaging in something that keeps you active also keeps your brain active. Engaging in exercise does not give time for your negative thoughts to crop up and take root. Ensuring that you are not idle means you no longer have time for the brain to drift to the sabotaging thoughts. When you stay active, you simply don't have time to think about the things that can go wrong or reasons you shouldn't finish a task. And once you complete your task of exercise, the rest of your list seems to be possible.

Exercise also releases positive feel good hormones like

endorphins. These can be a natural antidepressant, and the release of endorphins can be slow releasing, long-lasting throughout your day, long after the exercise is over.

Ensuring that you have enough rest is key to having energy for the next day. Rest and repair from effort today prepares you for the task ahead tomorrow. A well-rested mind and body can concentrate and engage in activities better. This is another area where routine and commitment pays off in creating a continuous loop. This is also a great time to meditate if you aren't in the habit yet of doing this in the morning.

Gratitude

Sometimes in the quest for a change in our lives, we tend to look at our current situations and decide that because we desire change, our circumstances as they are today being not worthy or desirable. In truth, if we harness the ability to separate those two, we are less prone to negative thinking. If you can remind yourself that you have parts of your life that are desirable and good, and you also simply want to meet new goals, your goals now no longer become a reflection of your life, as if you must meet your goals only and solely because your current life is not good enough.

For example, you can desire to lose weight and be more fit simply because it's a healthy goal, not because you can't "stand" your current weight. This kind of thinking tends towards self-hatred, low self-esteem and criticism, all of which set up those negative spirals that sabotage your goals. When you feel good about yourself, this is when you are most likely to stay committed. Even if you do assess your life and see areas of change, a neutral stance towards those areas is healthiest. You can notice and identify that you need to lose weight or finish your education or get a new job without hating or being critical of your current job, weight or educational levels.

When we also live in a state of deficiency, or at least perceive that we do, we have increased stress hormones. This is yet another biological, innate tendency as a survival mechanism. We are meant to seek out more when we feel we don't have enough. In survival terms, this usually relates to shelter or food, so our caveman brains see that we don't have enough of something, and determines that we must stress until we get more of it. The problem is that we often aren't stressing over survival based needs in this current day and age, but our brains don't know the difference. The more we can focus on what we do have, the more we are able to allow our stress to calm and our brains to stay in a state of neutral. We can focus on obtaining things we do want since we aren't coming from a state of deprivation and scarcity.

Make a list of daily grateful observances. These can be about self or others, but the practice of seeking positive instead of negative will always have positive outcomes.

Meditation

The Art of Disciplining Your Mind

The practice of meditation and mindfulness has the power to increase your willpower. Meditation and mindfulness both use the art of staying present in the moment without being prone to distraction or needing to avoid an emotion and serve to increase emotional awareness and intelligence.

Science also backs this up. Practicing mindfulness, even for 5 minutes per day, can increase the gray matter in your brain that is responsible for helping you control decision making and managing our emotions, especially impulses.

Stress and anxiety are often the downfalls of completing goals, and often these bring negative thoughts about ourselves that create the negative feedback loop. Meditation works to notice when those are happening and cancel them out. It releases feel good chemicals, just like exercise that can help reduce the stress hormones like cortisol that feed anxiety. Meditation and mindfulness reduce cravings and acting on impulses by calming the very hormones that feed those.

Not only does meditation help increase these hormones, it also helps the brain make actual connections in the neural pathways that either didn't exist or were not very strong. Think of the process of meditation as building highways in your brain. The longer you work on it, the more the highways can be built. Not only does it build better pathways in the brain for things like calm and control, it also reduces the highways that feed stress and fear. Think of it as rerouting traffic based simply on how you think. That traffic is the thoughts and internal experience that goes on all day long

One of the best parts about meditation is that it increases the sense of gratitude and less thoughts surrounding scarcity. It helps to clear the mind of fears or negative thoughts and reestablishes a healthy, centered thought pattern. It improves mental, emotional and physical focus all at once.

Meditation doesn't have to take long. It can be done before bed or when you wake up, in less than 15 minutes. Some people enjoy meditating on a topic, or by using a recording that helps keep their mind on a thought pattern. It can help your mind to stay focused on relaxation by listening to a speaker who guides you. Meditation can be guided by someone else or by also repeating a script in your mind. When your thoughts begin to wander, simply bring them back to the topic or to the present.

Mindfulness meditation is a mental discipline. It all begins with focus, either on your body, your breath or on a repeated thought. You simply observe all your thoughts, feelings, and changes that arise moment to moment. Like a boat in a stream, you observe them floating by without thinking too long or making judgments. You constantly bring the thoughts and awareness back to the here and now.

If you struggle with meditation and simply thinking calm thoughts, then try a focus on grounding. Grounding is focusing attention on your body and sensations in the here and now. Usually you can start with one of the 5 senses, and describe it in your brain in detail. Start with one that is pleasurable like taste and simply notice what it is like to taste a cup of coffee or tea. Then move to touch and touch a comforting item like a soothing blanket or putting on lotion. Meditation doesn't have to mean sitting still, but is simply about not allowing yourself to focus anywhere other than what is happening in the current moment and learning to embrace the current even if it's not pleasurable. This practice is part of what breaks the need to give into cravings or impulses when you feel anxious about completing a task.

You can also do a body scan, where you start at the top of your head, "check in" with how it feels, if there is any pressure, tightness, or sensation, and then move to your face. You can scrunch or tighten parts of your face, and then relax. Then move to shoulders, arms, hands and on down the rest of your body. For people who struggle to simply listen to their thoughts, engaging their body in grounding or body scans can be a much easier form of meditation and mindfulness.

Mindfulness is also about learning to practice tolerating discomfort for short periods of time to begin developing a natural ability to manage it. It's natural to avoid pain, but as we've said before, avoiding short term issues for an impulse means that long term pain is inevitable. Every distraction or impulse trains you to believe that you can't handle distress. Practice slowly feeling uncomfortable and verify that you are stronger than you may think. Start with one small action like running one minute longer than you normally do, or studying for 5 extra minutes before you check your phone. You can also mindfully eat your meal or observe a situation you normally distract from like a drive home. Turn off the radio and see what your drive feels like when you aren't engaging in thinking or listening elsewhere!

Using Affirmations

Researchers believe we seek out negative or dangerous information to avoid it, and these kinds of thoughts become our constant thinking patterns. We have survived based on the ability to detect and then avoid anything that is dangerous. Today that means that we sometimes make things overly negative to avoid failure. However, since our environment isn't as dangerous as that of a caveman, we can instead work towards at least a neutral stance, if not towards positive. Even though we naturally can seek negative risks, we can also control the kinds of thoughts the mind produces. And when you start one type of thinking, the rest of your thoughts tend to follow. You can program yourself and your mind to tend towards neutral or positive.

Mediation will assist you in learning how to keep a neutral stance on your thoughts. You can learn through the practice of being present to just simply observe all your thoughts. Instead of having to actively work on changing your negative thoughts, you can instead distance yourself and simply ignore them. Imagine them as boats on a stream. You can allow them to simply pass, and only pick up the boats that are positive and engaging. Observing that negative thoughts happen doesn't specify credit to them as realistic.

When you don't actively engage with those thoughts, they continue floating down the stream.

On the flip slide, you can introduce even more positive thoughts that put even more positive boats in the stream. The more of these you have, the more it crowds out the negative thoughts. Affirmations are seeking positive observances and being grateful. Affirmations are always self focused and are positive or neutral challenges to any negative self talk.

Here are some beginning ways to incorporate affirmations into your own mental self-talk:

> "I know how to say yes and no to the things that will move me forward today. I can work and

forgo distractions. I have all the skills I need to dedicate myself to committing to my goals and completing each of them".

"When I start working on a task or a goal, I visualize the ending and how I will be successful. I work towards that until the daily goal is done. I can work without distracting myself and I stick to my plans. I am a success".

"I recognize that in my past I sometimes didn't complete the task. There are always times today I could do the same. Today and every day I stay mindful through my meditations and mindfulness to recognize when I am starting down a distracted path. I am in tune with myself enough to know that I need to change and correct my course. I can direct my thoughts, emotions and energy back toward what matters most to me and I stay focused. I forgive myself easily of any missteps and get back to the matter at hand".

"Today I choose to commit to myself and my own happiness and whatever it takes to get there".

"Today I choose not to engage in self sabotaging behaviors"

"I have all the energy and direction I need to accomplish my desired goals"

The words that we say out loud or even internally are not reality. However, whatever we perceive to be the truth is reality for ourselves and we will act as if these things are true. We see ourselves and the world around us through the lens of our thoughts, and if those are negative, we are then prone to see the world in that same way. The way we talk to ourselves matters and without motivation from within in the form of positive affirmations and encouragements, we are doomed to tell ourselves that we will fail and that will become our truth. Positive people and mentors are helpful at catching negative talk and helping us correct that, but our most positive influence should always be ourselves.

The interesting thing about affirmations is that they themselves are a form of discipline. Just like engaging in healthy eating and exercise, this is a type of dedication, that if done daily, results in an improvement in discipline in other areas of life.

Goals

Defined goals give you a clear direction and daily actions to accomplish your goals. Willpower is not enough when you don't have a map to follow to meet your goals. The best way to create goals is the SMART system. This means your goals are Specific, Measurable, Attainable, Relevant and Timely.

A goal of "losing weight" isn't specific. "I want to lose 10 pounds" is specific, and something you can measure, is an attainable goal, is relevant to your goal of losing weight and can be done within a normal time frame. Goals require you to establish daily action steps that will turn into habits once you've started and enacted them routinely. We reach our goals by doing these daily or weekly steps. The more often a step is accomplished, the more it becomes a habit. A habit repeated becomes routines. Routines are what we need to meet goals. To overcome procrastination and laziness, we must seek to make changes that are easier to follow and continue using over time. Anything we implement as a habit is easier to follow and less likely to be given to distraction or temptation.

Goals are accomplished by simply creating a list of behaviors that make up good habits. These are just as hard to break as bad habits! It is usually easiest to set some long-term goals, big "final" goals, like graduating or losing a certain large weight. Then you define the needed smaller goals in chunks, like you need to engage in monthly, weekly, and daily goals. Then set the behaviors needed to reach those that are also able to help you track your progress towards your goals.

It's important to review or look over your short and long term goals each morning and every evening. If you aren't assessing your work against your goals, you can easily get off track. This also helps you to reprioritize anything on your list that needs to change or be re-evaluated.

When you do plan your tasks or work, it's important to know what is most important so you can plan sufficiently. Start with the most important and get it out of the way first. Not only does this mean the most important tasks are handled, but it also ensures that the things you tend to procrastinate are already done first.

Organization and Time Management

Organization is crucial to accomplishing your tasks. The behaviors you encourage and the habits you implement reflect the value of organization and commitment to your goals.

So, while looking at your goals, ask yourself:

> What do I currently do that will need to change regarding organization?
>
> What time management issues do I have that distract me easily?
>
> What distractions can I turn into measurable rewards?

An organized operational life is a disciplined approach to life. If you are totally overwhelmed starting with your goals, then start with something physical in your space that you can organize. Begin by organizing one small area or definable place, like your desk or a drawer or even your closet. Move on to something else the next day. You may discover that you need an organized external life to focus yourself internally and avoid procrastination.

We also need to be able to prioritize the tasks and daily needs to meet the goals we want to accomplish. Each of us has the same 24 hours, and we must organize our time in a way that makes room for the stuff that matters. To meet our ending goals, we must rank the things in our day by important or urgency.

One way to do this is to make a quadrant and rank our daily needs. You label each quadrant with Urgent/Important, Not Urgent but Important, Important but Not Urgent, and then the time wasters and distractions that go in the Not Urgent and Not Important category. It helps to do all four since this also shows you how much time or effort you put into category 4, especially since these are wasters. You can also rank your "need to complete" activities and spread them throughout the day if this is less stressful. Choose the hardest tasks on your list that also have the highest priority, and do those first thing in the morning before any other distractions can get in your way.

The Pomodoro technique is an awesome way to manage time and those who are prone to distraction. It helps power through hard tasks by breaking them into manageable time portions. If too much time is overwhelming, this technique allows you to work in bursts while taking frequent breaks. It was created by a man who needed to work in short bursts, and he grabbed a tomato shaped kitchen timer, thus the name Pomodoro (Italian for Tomato!).

Here's how it works:

> Pick a task
>
> Set the timer to a period, start with 15 minutes if you are beginning the process.
>
> Work until the timer rings and then put a check mark or smiley face on a piece of paper.
>
> Take a short break, no longer than 5 minutes.

Do these 4 times to complete a Pomodoro and get 4 check marks or smiley faces. If you've worked in this manner, you can achieve a good bit in a little over an hour. After 4 check marks, take a longer break.

You don't have to do the same task to work on a Pomodoro. If you need to check emails, and make a phone call, both can be done in the time slot. It may be helpful in these cases to make a list of all you need to accomplish in manageable chunks.

Remember however that this method is meant to keep you productive but not handcuffed. Remain flexible! If you're finding that you are working hard and making good progress, and the timer goes off, you don't have to immediately stop. Find a natural stopping point and finish. The goal is all about helping you feel like your time is manageable and flexible within boundaries.

Commitment

There are a few ways to ensure that you are committed to the end process towards a goal and to stopping yourself from distraction or failure. One of those ways is what is called "burning the ships". Warriors would often burn their ships once they reached enemy shore to motivate themselves to fight even when they were exhausted, because they knew there were no other options than winning. There is no option to retreat! Sometimes in goals, like weight loss, people will "burn the ships" by getting rid of all their clothes that don't fit once they lose weight so they can't turn back.

Social commitment is the term used when you announce your goal to others to have more accountability. Do you have a situation or ending goal that you are seeking that can force you into action by burning the ships? Do you need to tell everyone about your goal for accountability so you can't back out? What strategies can you implement that will help you to commit to meeting the final goal?

Commitment to a goal or plan is a choice, and is a step towards discipline. The difference in commitment and learning discipline is that there is no anxiety or negative emotions with commitment. You simply choose the action or plan and decide to continue that daily. There isn't a balance between good or bad foods, choosing to be lazy or doing homework, but instead adopts a neutral stance that a choice is made and will continue to be made. For example, you don't hesitate to continue to commit to basic needs like maintaining your hygiene. You don't wake up and debate if you'll do these things, and if you should choose them, but instead you take out the options, and you naturally know at this point that choosing to complete the task is better for you in the long run.

Commitment is the choice to do a task or goal daily. The decision to do this and continue doing this is what leads to discipline! If you aren't sure where to start, the same advice is true with commitment. Start small, and start with one thing. If you struggle with any commitment, start small. Start today doing all the little things you know you should do, but don't feel like doing.

Changing your style of motivation and living is done slowly and with progressive commitment. The people who are most successful with any kind of change take it slow. They start with baby steps. They pick one thing each day to change. The thing they pick tomorrow may be the same thing they picked today, and they commit to choosing it daily until it's an automatic commitment.

Commitment is different from motivation. Motivation is often inspiring; however, it works from a hypothesis that you must be inspired or feel good before you can work. This means that you are chasing external sources of positive emotions to do your job. This is not enough. Commitment comes from within and is an internal inspiration to keep to your tasks.

Ask yourself:

> What am I hanging on to "in case I fail"?
>
> Are my backup plans in case of emergency, or are they allowing me to give up easily?
>
> Is there a negative consequence if I quit?
>
> What do I need to do to burn the boats in my situation?
>
> How can I make safety nets that don't let me give up?

Chapter 4

Don't Be a Perfectionist

This may sound like the opposite of the previous chapter, but despite the commitment to structure having impulse control, there isn't an expectation to be perfect and never slip or make mistakes.

One of the other major tenets that goes along with emotional intelligence that we discussed earlier is not only the ability to avoid impulses as it relates to avoiding emotions, but also the ability to stay balanced. Those with emotional intelligence can detect when their emotions or thoughts are irrational and not contributing to their overall well-being. So, when they struggle to meet a goal or task and they find themselves saying negative statements like "I should have done better" or I'm never going to meet this goal" they are able to see the negative impact these kinds of thoughts have on their mood and thoughts. A person attuned to their own internal emotions will be able to self-correct to prevent from sliding into many negative thoughts in a downward spiral.

A consistent ongoing environment of negative thoughts

about yourself does not motivate anyone to work harder on those goals or tasks, and instead only serves to pull that person into a spiral of negative thoughts about their abilities, and sabotage of their motivations to complete tasks. I know that the idea of whipping yourself into submission seems like it makes sense at first glance.

If you think that somehow reminding yourself over and over that you need to not fail, and need to remember not to "mess up" should push you to notice mistakes and avoid them. Instead it creates an environment of self-doubt, fear and sadness. Anyone who lives in an environment of doubt isn't likely to push through other negative emotions and will give into impulses and temptations to quit more often, because now they are experiencing the negative environment of self-doubt and anxiety on top of the uncomfortable feelings of stress over the work of a project or the need to sacrifice time out with friends to study. Adding more intense negative emotions to the mix does not make things easier, and in fact is a form of sabotage

Forgiving yourself and simply noticing where you can make changes, from a natural perspective, is much healthier and keeps you on task much longer. Accomplishing big things doesn't usually follow a simple straight line. Mistakes are also learning opportunities instead of failures. Learning from each of your mistakes and making new commitments to change continue to build self-discipline.

Chapter 5

Creating a Support Network

Success doesn't happen alone. In fact, most success stories depend on a rally of friends and family who were all able to help keep the succeeding person on track. There are always several factors that contribute to changing behaviors and meeting goals, but personal improvement because of positive people really cannot be minimized.

Positive influences by obvious default will have a positive impact! People who intend to see you succeed will support your efforts towards goals and can help keep you on track when you want to stop or sabotage yourself. Positive influencers are the type of people who will ask you if you're done studying when you ask if they want to go out for the night. Or they will ask you how you are meeting your goals a month after you tell them that you have big plans you want to accomplish.

It never hurts to have people cheering you on! We know from research that people who attempt marathons are more likely to complete the run if there are supportive cheerleaders along the way, even if this isn't their first time to run.

One interesting secret is if you want to know the average income of a person, look at their 7 closest friends or confidants. Same with almost anything else in their lives. Are they successful at work? Able to be trusted? Just look at their support system for your answers. Research says that we become a mirror of the 7 people in our lives that we interact with the most, so ask yourself if your 7 people help you toward that goal. If you surveyed their lives, do they look like the life you want? Or are they made up of actions and outcomes that are failures or that don't reflect the path you want to be on?

Positive influencers aren't always necessarily those who simply cheer you on and give you nothing but positive feedback. In fact, sometimes they are the ones who push you the hardest and might give you the most criticism. Helpful criticism of course, but direct observance of things you must change nonetheless! Those who will help you stay accountable don't always make things feel good but since they also have the eye on the end goal that you've proclaimed you want, they assist you in not going towards that short term, feel good impulses and direct you back towards the harder efforts that will pay off in the end.

Positive people are often not jealous of your successes and will cheer you on, even if you surpass them in happiness, relationships or income. These people are the ones who are the most supportive towards achieving your goals. They are ok helping you feel good about yourself and your plans, because they focus the same efforts towards themselves and life in general. They have applied meditation, gratitude and positive thinking on their own plans and are now in the habit of doing this with themselves and other people. They have a strong sense of who they are and what works, and they have good self-esteem. Because they've done the hard work of repairing their negative thoughts, they also can do the same for you.

To succeed in meeting those daily and weekly tasks, you must have confidence that the amount of work and sacrifice will pay off. Sometimes that also includes putting yourself out there to make big changes that can rattle your friends and family. By nature, we as humans are averse to risk and we enjoy things that seem stable and routine. Supportive people can see your changes and risks, and give you supportive encouragement instead of tearing down your plans because it makes them uncomfortable. Positive people recognize that not all change is risky, and that not all risk is something to avoid.

Here are some of the types of positive and encouraging people you should keep in your corner:

1. The Hard Worker. This person has the abilities

that you are desiring to develop. They are the kind of person that could write this book or the kind who has the very outcome you are working towards today. They are the relentless worker, who doesn't give into procrastination and may even be a little bit of a mystery to you. They are the type of person who can measure their own progress and not feel deflated if they make a mistake or don't meet a goal instantly. Instead they take all feedback as useful and meaningful and know how to turn a mistake into learning options. They are usually passionate about their own success but have no problem being passionate about supporting yours as well. They can give critical feedback, but often their feedback is easier to receive since you know it comes from a place of experience. They also have action steps you can implement once they give critical feedback that will tell you what to change and how to change it. It can be easier to hear their criticism since you may want what they have and are willing to hear what you are currently doing wrong so that you can eventually get it right.

2. Cheerleaders: These people tend to be positive and in a state of calm gratitude, either naturally or by effort. They are generally happy even when circumstances are difficult, and they can be inspirational. They inspire creativity and they

push you when you feel like quitting.

3. Curious innovators: since nothing is ever outside of the realm of possibility for these scientific minded people, they have no problem accepting if you have an innovative or seemingly risky idea. They are motivated by asking "what if it works" and finding out how to make something successful. They approach life and business in a scientific mode, but they are emotionally passionate about this approach and can be like a cheerleader, who pushes you on to try something that may seem hard or scary. They constantly ask themselves how they can grow and change and try all manner of options to make it towards a successful end goal. They also have no problem with failure as they simply see it as one stepping stone towards success. These kinds of people can approach situations from multiple angles and options and can help you overcome hurdles with new ideas.

4. Idealists. There are people that are visionary idealists, who can remain hopeful about ideas or circumstances that might scare others. To keep this drive going, we should always be surrounding ourselves with people who have similar goals in mind. These dreamers don't even need to be involved in the same industry as you or your business; the important thing is that you

keep close people with big plans for themselves. Seeing other people's drive will keep you hungry to reach your goals.

Think about that list of people we mentioned earlier and ask yourself if they are positive and supportive people.

> Do they make you feel like you have what it takes to reach your goals?

> Do they support you?

> Do they make you feel worthy or able to meet your goals?

> Do you feel better, encouraged or energized after spending time with them?

If you can answer yes, then you are likely surrounded by the people who are most supportive. If you feel like you need to attract new support, you'll do best if you can remember that positive people are often attracted to other positive people. You must exhibit positive thoughts and emotions, and over all be confident. Negativity only holds you back!

Chapter 6

Making Things Pleasurable and Fun!

One of the cool things that may continue to motivate you towards becoming more disciplined is learning that people who are able to master these skills turn out to be happier in general! Self-discipline isn't about simply avoiding things that feel temporarily good, but also about being able to avoid things that eventually make you feel worse. Disciplined people can think farther ahead and see that acting on a whim causes a cascade of negative outcomes and that these negative outcomes will have a sense of lack of control and less happiness.

Disciplined people can see two conflicting situations: desire to complete a task that is hard vs desire to quit and do fun things. Research has found a strong correlation between those that complete tasks and can stay dedicated to those tasks and higher satisfaction in life. This seems quite intuitive as those people also tend to accomplish things that improve their life. Research also shows that the ability to stick to completing tasks means less influence by negative emotions at all and more time feeling positive or calm.

These people weren't better able to resist an impulse or temptation, but rather were better at designing a life that didn't introduce as many of those temptations in the first place. They were better at crafting a life situation that didn't include those cravings, distractions or sabotaging behaviors. Instead of simply "being stronger" than others, those who are disciplined just avoid finding themselves in situations that create conflict with their stated goals.

But what if you really do thrive off fun? Let's work that into your goals as well! Nobody said that discipline had to be sacrifice and pain with no reward. We simply need to remove rewards that turn into distractions for yourself.

Start by making a list of rewards you enjoy. After you list the things that feel rewarding, ask yourself:

> Do these ever take me away from my goals, like a piece of candy when I'm trying to lose weight?
>
> Do I struggle to moderate this if I engage in it?

If you answer yes to either of those two situations, they will be short term rewards that turn into long term distractions. If they don't distract, then feel free to use them! An example is using the Pomodoro technique we talked about earlier. At the end of each dedicated time, you can have a treat, if you aren't prone to overeating. Or if you still want that reward, portion out an exact amount and put the rest far away from where you are working. Or if social media is your reward, then set a new timer for your reward time and set a commitment to stop when the timer is up. If you find that you try a reward and you can't stop or stay distracted, it's time to make that your FINAL ending reward once you finish the task. This way your work is already done, and since it's a one-time reward and not something you keep doing intermittently until the task is done, you may find it easier to moderate.

You can also find that the very things that motivate you are also fun! Motivation is typically a positive emotion, that comes with a surge of excitement. Do you need to watch motivational video's every day? Follow people on social media who inspire you? Listen to songs as you work that help you feel energized to work or complete a workout? The nice thing about motivating yourself is that you don't find it to be an energy drain! The very things that motivate you may jump start you each day to complete your tasks!

Never forget as well that the product of your work will be reward, but that can also be true daily. Your ability to go out and have fun is even more of a reward when done after completing tasks that make you feel accomplished!

If you can see dedication and discipline as motivating and invigorating instead of draining and a pain, you can find it far more engaging and easier to do! It all goes back to that positive internal mindset that you enjoy this work and you can do hard things.

Conclusion

The process of change from impulsive procrastinator to goal accomplisher means making an internal change that includes learning and growth. This helps transform who we are how we see ourselves, others, circumstances and how we interact with the world around us.

If you still aren't sure where to start, then begin with these small tips to jump start you:

Pick at least 5 things you can get done tomorrow. If you really were committed to making change and proving to yourself that you are capable, you can power through almost anything. Begin with 5 things, even those that have nothing to do with your ending goal, and do them within 24 hours.

Start with positive thinking and mindfulness to stay in the present moment. Nothing is as destructive to goals as negative thoughts and sabotaging yourself. You really can't ever go wrong by learning how to harness your mind. Even if you don't jump start your disciplined life today, you can improve your emotions and thoughts immediately with a new focus.

One of the most important things to truly change your habits from laziness to discipline is to approach the change from a viewpoint of positive addition instead of punitive subtraction. What that means is to think about one thing you will add to your day instead of something you are giving up or letting go. People who change their eating habits positively are more able to change when they view their eating habits as adding in more protein, or adding in more nutrients via leafy greens. They see the addition of more control, or the ability to feel better after eating.

To approach change from a positive, addition stand point makes you automatically begin to feel as if you are receiving instead of losing. On the other hand, those who approach change by thinking of what they must give up, like time or "favorite foods", feel deprived. Deprivation is never a good motivator to stick to long term, healthy change! Start today by making a list of all the ways you will feel enhanced immediately by adding in these new behaviors. Maybe you'll feel less stressed. Or you'll feel physically better from sticking to a health routine. Begin to see yourself in this new life by visualizing yourself as a disciplined person and begin acting today as if this is true.

It's never too late to start this process. It doesn't matter if you weigh a certain amount, or have waited until a certain age to begin a degree- time is going to pass whether you begin this new journey, so time and "being too late" are all irrelevant. Where will you be in 5 years? Those 5 years are going to pass, how will you wish you spent that time? Nobody is keeping score or watching to ensure that you have perfection. Most people are busy living their own lives and aren't all that preoccupied with what is happening in ours. Other than our supportive cheerleaders, nobody is out there watching to see if we succeed or fail. They don't expect us to make it by a certain time, and there is no scorekeeper waiting to see if we are able to complete the race in record time. Start making changes, but go at a pace that you can continue without burning out and sabotaging yourself.

No matter what, your life will improve the second you commit to having a better-disciplined life!

Part 2

Habits

How to Implement Essential Habits to Improve Productivity, Success and Wealth

Spence Adams

The contents of this book may not be reproduced, duplicated or transmitted without direct written permission from the author.
Under no circumstances will any legal responsibility or blame be held against the publisher for any reparation, damages, or monetary loss due to the information herein, either directly or indirectly.

Legal Notice:

This book is copyright protected. This is only for personal use. You cannot amend, distribute, sell, use, quote or paraphrase any part or the content within this book without the consent of the author.

Disclaimer Notice:

Please note the information contained within this document is for educational and entertainment purposes only. Every attempt has been made to provide accurate, up to date and reliable complete information. No warranties of any kind are expressed or implied. Readers acknowledge that the author is not engaging in the rendering of legal, financial, medical or professional advice. The content of this book has been derived from various sources. Please consult a licensed professional before attempting any techniques outlined in this book.

By reading this document, the reader agrees that under no circumstances are is the author responsible for any losses, direct or indirect, which are incurred as a result of the use of information contained within this document, including, but not limited to, —errors, omissions, or inaccuracies.

© Copyright 2017 Dibbly Publishing.
All rights reserved.

Table of Contents

Introduction 1

Chapter 1 What Is A Habit? 3
   Your Past 3
   Your Present 5
   Your Future 8

Chapter 2 Which Habits Matter Most – Specific Keystone Habits To Be Successful 11
   Financial Keystone Habits 13
   Relationships 14
   Productivity 15
   Fitness 15
   Staying Mentally Sharp 16

Chapter 3 Mindset For Building Good Habits 19

Chapter 4 How To Change Your Bad Habits To Good Habits 23
   List All The Bad Habits That You Need To Change 23

Chapter 5 8 Elements Of A Habit Stacking Routine . 29

Chapter 6 Useful Life Habits 35
   Habit #20 35
   Habit #21 37
   Habit #22 39
   Habit #23 41
   Habit #24 42
   Habit #25 44
   Habit #26 45
   Habit #27 47
   From Here, Where Do You Go? 49

Chapter 7 What Do Successful People Avoid? 51
   What Successful People Avoid 51

Chapter 8 Creating Big Goals For Success 59

Chapter 9 Habits That Lead To Success 63
HABIT #28 63
HABIT #29 64
HABIT #30 65
HABIT #31 65
HABIT #32 66
HABIT #33 66
HABIT #34 67
HABIT #35 67
HABIT #36 68

Chapter 10 Good Habits To Improve Your Health .. 69
HABIT #37 69
HABIT #38 70
HABIT #39 71
HABIT #40 71
HABIT #41 72
HABIT #42 72
HABIT #43 72
HABIT #44 73
HABIT #45 73

Chapter 11 How Good Habits Can Change Your Life? 75

Chapter 12 Finding Time To Relax 79

Chapter 13 Productivity At Work 81

Chapter 14 Habits To Improve Your Finances 83
HABIT #46 83
HABIT #47 84
HABIT #48 84
HABIT #49 85

Chapter 15 Daily Habits That Can Help You Increase Your Level Of Self-Discipline 87
HABIT #50 87
HABIT #51 89

HABIT #52	89
HABIT #53	90
HABIT #54	91
HABIT #55	92
HABIT #56	93
HABIT #57	95

Chapter 16 The Reasons You Have Trouble Creating Good Habits 97

Chapter 17 Surround Yourself With Positive People ...101

HABIT #58	101
HABIT #59	102
HABIT #60	102
HABIT #61	104

Chapter 18 Tips To Getting The Habit To Stick 107

Conclusion 113

Introduction

Do you want to start a good habit? Has it been a struggle for you to let go of a bad habit? If so, then you need to read this book right now.

Building a collection of good habits is the only way to stay productive. Unfortunately, many people do not know how to get rid of their bad habits and replace them with good ones. This book has all the answers you need to start good habits that you need to achieve the success you want in life.

In this book, you will get to understand how habits work. You will also discover the top habits you and everyone else needs in life to become productive and successful. Most importantly, you will learn ten tested-and-proven techniques that will help you build any habit you want.

Whether you are a student struggling to maintain study habits, an office worker trying to climb the corporate ladder, a work-from-home entrepreneur who wants to establish a productive routine, or a retiree who wishes to learn a new skill, this book is for you.

Chapter 1

What is a Habit?

For most people, habits are activities that we do without thinking too much about them. When a choice or activity seems to come naturally, we call it a habit.

More technical definitions of a habit come from scientists who research the psychological and physical aspects of habits. When scientists study habits, they tend to determine whether or not some choice or activity is a habit based on the subject's PAST, PRESENT, and FUTURE track record with respect to the choice or activity in question.

Your Past

People who define habits based upon the past will look at repetition and frequency. They believe, essentially, that if you do something enough times, it automatically becomes a habit.

They also take frequency of the activity into consideration. Frequency brings some set amount of time into the mix. It's not just that you've done the activity 100 times – it's that you've done it 100 times in

10 days, or 100 days in a row, or some other regular period of time.

There are problems with defining habits solely by repetition and/or frequency, though. Namely, individual differences. The number of times and/or frequency can be different for different people and different tasks. If you assume that on the 29th day of doing something, it's magically something you will do forever from now on, you might give up when you needed more time or commitment to really make it a hardened habit.

You might think that you have to start all over if you miss a day or two here and there. You might also encounter problems doing away with or replacing bad habits if you think only in terms of repetition and frequency.

For the most part, however, habits do often take hold simply by repeating a behavior or thought over and over. Your mind learns to anticipate the habit after a long time of consistent repetition. Your body then learns to expect to repeat behaviors.

Muscle memory is a great example. If you've ever participated in a sport (or even video games, knitting, cooking - anything where you learn a specific physical technique to do something), you've probably discovered that your body tends to automatically put itself in the position that you've taught it.

That's true even when the original positioning seemed very odd or uncomfortable when you first learned and tried it.

The only problem is that pesky fact that there is lots of individual difference between humans. Studies show us that forming habits from repetition is different from person to person.

When someone tells you that you need to do something 21 or 28 or 80 times to make it a habit, take it with a grain of salt. Their particular number of repetitions might be true for some people, but that definitely does not mean it's true for everyone!

Some of the studies also show that some people can create habits very quickly. Others often take several months. There are even some people who find that it takes years to develop certain habits with repetition alone.

But, take heart and don't worry! I had a really hard time developing habits, so I have plenty of tricks and tips that I learned to help myself go beyond simply repeating an action and hoping that it sticks. I'll share those with you here.

Your Present

Some of the psychological studies that look at the subject of habits look for something called "automaticity." They use that word to describe when a choice or activity feels almost automatic to the person involved.

Automaticity happens when the person experiences only lower-level thoughts during the active experience of that habit.

So those people would identify habits based on the amount of thought you give to the choice or activity.

There are, of course, exceptions to this rule. Consider habits that cause a lot of psychological distress. For example, smokers might give a lot of thought to their activity...

- They might feel weak that they find it difficult to stop.

- They probably consider the addictiveness of tobacco.

- They might feel discomfort or even shame when doing the activity in appropriate areas or in front of other people.

- They might think about the habit when not actively performing the habit because of side effects, including medical conditions.

Then there are the habits that require more complex thoughts or concentration.

For instance, if you drive to work every day, your tasks and route might feel automatic. The activity is more complex and involves more of your conscious attention.

Even though you might have days where you don't quite remember the act of driving to work, you probably use more than just low-level thought processes while actually doing the driving. It's inherent in the nature of the act. It requires more involvement from you to be done at all.

When I talk about habits, I tend to combine choices and activities. We will talk later, however, about an important difference between habits that deal with decisions and habits that involve specific activities.

There are times when general choices and mindsets become habits. Habits can be as simple as consistently thinking a certain way in similar circumstances.

Understanding that thoughts can be habits, too, will help you immensely when it comes to understanding your habits, breaking bad habits, and developing good new habits.

Automatically thinking certain ways without internal debate or doubt has the potential to be good or bad. It's important to understand the "automatic" part of habits to be able to recognize and change mindsets that promote and maintain some of your bad habits.

Your Future

Some studies base the definition of habit on the likelihood of you repeating the action in the future.

In theory, this is a good way to think of a habit. It's usually based on how many times you've performed the thought or action in the past. It also takes into consideration how automatic the thought or action is while you do it. In other words, how likely you are to think or do something without consciously deciding to do so.

In addition, most studies that try to predict continued habits rely on psychological aspects surrounding the potential habit. This includes any psychological and/or physical rewards and punishments received as a result of repeating the habit, as well as the complexity of the habit itself (and other related factors).

However, there are problems with defining a habit based on future expectations, as well. The past might not matter as much as one believes. Sometimes people continue bad habits despite bad consequences. And, some simple habits can easily be dropped.

Like anything else people try to predict, there is a certain amount of chaos involved:

- Your best intentions can go awry.

- Other people can thwart you.
- Unexpected changes can occur.

There are a lot of reasons why things that seem likely to occur might end up not happening.

As you can see, the definition of a habit from an objective perspective can be vague and complex. Simply saying that something is a habit once you've done it 28 times doesn't apply to every action or person. It isn't nearly that simple!

You really are the best judge of whether or not a thought or action is a habit. And only you can say for certain when a thought or action crosses the threshold and becomes a full-blown habit. There is no one-size-fits-all when it comes to this determination.

The past, present, and future guidelines for how habits generally work are good, basic criteria. They will help you realize that something is a bad habit or when something becomes a good habit. But beyond that, it isn't wise to put too much stock in this means of determining a habit's status. At least not as the end point in that process.

If you've repeated the thought or action many times on a regular basis, it feels comfortable (almost automatic) to you, and you're fairly sure you're going to do it again tomorrow, it has probably become a habit. At this point, that's the best anyone can say with any real assurance.

Chapter 2

Which Habits Matter Most – Specific Keystone Habits to Be Successful

Keystone habits are the most important habits. These foundation habits are the ones that will directly impact your goals and your life. They are the habits upon which you will build all other new habits. They are the habits that can change your perspective and break you out of ruts. They are the habits that you need to succeed – bottom line.

Your keystone habits should be based on your overall goals. When you repeat these important habits, you should always feel like you're taking positive steps toward reaching your most important life goals.

Please note that, just because the goals are important, that doesn't mean they have to be big. Mini habits that work toward your goals and help inspire big mindset changes within you are a perfect example. It only takes a few minutes each day, but the results add up.

Establishing even one keystone habit will help you understand what other habits you need to create, which habits are holding you back, and which habits are basically neutral. I can't stress too much how important these bedrock habits will become in your life!

Before you create some new habit just to see if you can make something a habit, think about the biggest goal that you want to achieve.

- Will the new potential habit constitute even a small step toward achieving your goal?

- Will the habit still be worth doing once you start to achieve your goal?

- Is the habit the opposite of some other existing habit that you might need to replace?

Remember that not all bad habits are necessarily detrimental. The big bad habits that you do need to get rid of are the ones that make you work against your overall goals. That's the measuring stick.

Will you be able to add more mini habits to your keystone habits to create a progressive routine based on making positive life changes? You will once you establish a keystone habit. It will guide your future actions, including habits you try to build.

Let's take a look at some examples of important keystone habits in different aspects of life. Your particular keystone habits will, of course, depend upon your specific overall goals.

Financial Keystone Habits

Obviously, most financial goals are based on saving money and/or making money. Some good examples of fundamental mini habits here would include:

Habit #1

Spending five minutes each day working on a side business, invention, or potentially money-making idea.

Habit #2

Taking five minutes each day to know exactly how much money you have and check on any upcoming necessary expenses.

Habit #3

Checking out one possible investment each day until you find one that shows promise.

Habit #4

Reading one article a day on money matters.

Relationships

Some life-changing mini habits when it comes to relationships might include:

Habit #5

Thinking about one thing that happened the previous day and consciously giving your partner the benefit of the doubt until you train your brain to automatically do so.

Habit #6

Recalling ONE important detail of the last conversation you had with your partner (it's a good way to pay more attention and remember things that matter to your significant other).

Habit #7

Spending five minutes thinking of something nice that you can do or say that day – and actually doing or saying it.

Habit #8

Smiling at your partner once a day – actual smile, no smirking.

Productivity

Habit #9
Make a to-do list of at least 3 achievable tasks at the start of each day.

Habit #10
Send an email or post to valuable contacts every day (or work on acquiring such contacts for 5 minutes each day).

Habit #11
Spend 5 minutes on a task that you just began before you have a chance to procrastinate.

Habit #12
When you're ready to end your workday, spend 5 more minutes on a task.

Fitness

Habit #13
Wear clothing and shoes that remind you of your goals and encourage you to be more active throughout your day (when possible).

Habit #14

Do 5 sit-ups, push-ups, squat thrusts, or minutes on an exercise machine each day.

Habit #15

Thoroughly stretch before getting into the shower, sitting down at your desk, or some other daily activity.

Habit #16

Put on a fast song and dance in your chair for the duration.

Staying mentally sharp

Habit #17

Do one thing differently each day – taking a different route, using a different greeting, wearing different clothing, eating something new at your favorite restaurant, etc.

Habit #18

Do one logic problem, math problem, word game or another challenging activity.

Habit #19

Make up a story – give dialogue when you watch people,

think of some scenario involving an adventure for your car, or take 5 minutes thinking about the best superpower you could possibly have and what you'd do with it.

While keystone habits might seem insignificant, they are the little habits that can help you make progress toward the big changes that you want to see happen in your life. All it takes is a small change in your mindset or routine, consistently practiced on a regular basis.

Figure out which daily tasks will have an impact and which won't. Drop the ones that are doing actual harm or keeping you from achieving what you want. Ignore the ones that don't matter, and create habits that will make a difference.

Remember, this is a process. It will take some trial-and-error. Don't let the inevitable setbacks upset or derail your efforts!

Chapter 3

Mindset for Building Good Habits

One of the reasons why people have a hard time breaking bad habits is that they fail to adopt the right mindset. Forming a good habit requires a new perspective, so it does not help to use the same way of thinking. What's on your mind when you bring you work home with you every night. Do you continued to think about your work when you are with your wife and children? Are you more of an absent parent then a present parent? If you want to be a more present parent, then you need to avoid the same train of thought. Though you may have already settled with fruit juices and milk teas for a healthier lifestyle, giving in to feelings of frustration may cause you to grab a burger at the first opportunity and revive old behavioral patterns.

To form good habits, a positive and open mindset may be in order. To arrive at that ideal way of thinking, shape your thoughts in these directions:

1. Replacing bad habits is about returning to your original state. We think that forming good habits

is about overhauling ourselves. The truth is you do not have to be a different person to break your bad habits. Bad habits are acquired, which means you originally functioned without them. The key is to figure out when the habit formed. Was there an additional stressor that was added to your life? Was there another habit that the current habit replaced? You were functioning well before the habit was created so you certainly can function without it.

2. You are so much more than your bad habits. Some people think that they are their bad habits. Hence, the transformation. These bad habits should not define you. We must understand that individuals are imperfect and human existence has always been a series of trials, errors and lessons learned. Repetitive bad behavior is nothing more but a testament to human imperfection, while overcoming it is proof that humanity can always be better.

3. You are a work in progress. Another sure recipe for failure is to keep dwelling on your disadvantages. If you focus on your strengths and work on realistic goals, you can speed up the formation of new habits. You may fail once in a while, but everyone has had their fair share of failures. You may be overweight at present, but that does not mean you cannot lose weight in

three months' time. Always give yourself a pat on the back and remember that if others succeeded, then you will too.

4   Just take it easy. You do not have to be so hard on yourself. Take a breather every now and them. Set up a cheat day (time when you can return to old habits) if you must but do not forget the reason why you need to form a healthier routine. Of course, this does not apply to every bad habit. Be mindful of how harmful the habit is on you, your family and your life. Most habits won't hurt you in moderation, as mentioned earlier in the book, the habit is formed in your subconscious and is not easily removed. Some habits might be better left not recalled. Anticipate your mistakes so you do not have to feel bad whenever you commit one. Bounce back and press on until you find a strategy that works.

5   What you are doing is meaningful. Some people fail to change their habits because they do not believe something worthwhile can come out of it. You must trust in the process. Do not think that changing a habit is something you cannot do. Believe that your efforts will pay off in the end. After your struggles to change for the better, you can become a stronger and more capable person.

Chapter 4

How to Change Your Bad Habits to Good Habits

List All the Bad Habits That You Need to Change

You probably have a list of bad habits to change when you bought this book. Those are the bad habits that you wanted to change because it does not help you or it does not contribute to your well-being at all. Most people, when asked about their bad habits, automatically think of the worst habits they have like gambling, binge drinking, smoking, etc. The steps in this book will help you change those habits too, of course, but aside from those, you also have to examine other things that you repeatedly do every day.

It would be best to make a list of the habits that you want to change. You cannot change all of them at once, so you have to tackle each one carefully. Now, aside from the bad habits mentioned above, what other habits do you have that are not helping you?

People have three types of habits:

> **Good habits** – Just like the ones practiced by the people in the last chapter, these habits help people do their work and become more creative and productive. These habits enhance their lives and provide them with good and lasting results.
>
> **Bad habits** – These habits are destructive to one's health and career. These are the habits that pull people downward slowly, until they realize that it was too late to do anything about it.
>
> **Mannerisms** – These are behaviors that do not really affect people negatively or positively. These are the little gestures that people do just because they got used to it. When you scratch the back of your neck if you're asked a question that you don't know the answer to, or when you bite your lip before saying anything, you do not really cause harm to yourself or to other people. Mannerisms can be changed, but because it is also a habit, it cannot be fully eliminated. There is no need to change it anyway, especially if you didn't get in trouble because of it.

What you need to focus on are the bad habits. To start your habit transformation, you need to list down all of the bad habits that you are aware of. These are the habits that you want to change as soon as you can because they affect you in highly negative ways. You can call this list the Primary list, because you will be dealing with them first.

Next, you need to look at your bad habits and see whether there are other bad habits that you do right after doing the items in the Primary list. For example, if you are smoking, do you automatically reach out for a gum or candy afterward? In that case, that behavior is a bad habit too, because if you are a chronic smoker, then you put as much sugar in your mouth as you do nicotine. Another example is if you are a gambler, and you automatically call someone to borrow money right after you lose — then borrowing is another habit. List all the habits that you do that come after the primary habit. Call this list your Secondary one.

Lastly, list all the habits that you can think of that cause unpleasant things in your life right now. This will be a bit trickier than the first two lists, because you need to think from the results to the cause. Most of the things in this list will come to you as a habit because you may not acknowledge it as so. However, remember that everything that happens in your life finds its roots in the things that you do consistently. So, to find the habits that should be included in this list, you have to think of the exact things that cause your problems.

You can do this by asking yourself why for each problem

that you have. For example:

- You have spent many years in your job but you're still not promoted. Why?
- Because people who are close to the boss get promoted first. Why?
- Because the boss like these people. Why?
- Because they provide good work. Why?
- Because they meet their targets. Why?
- Because they show up on time and do their work earnestly.

Keep asking yourself why until you find an answer that cannot be questioned anymore. In the example above, you are attributing your problem to external factors.

Now, try replacing any mention of external factors and replace it with yourself:

- You have spent many years in your job but you're still not promoted. Why?
- Because people who are close to the boss get promoted first. Why?
- Because the boss doesn't like me. Why?

- Because I do not do my work to his or her expectations. Why?

- Because I do not feel like doing it. Why?

- Because I'd rather spend my time having fun. Why?

- Because I hate my job. Why?

You will find that you might go around in circles when you do this. This is still because you still think that your problems are caused by other people. If this happens, take a step back and look at it closely. Do you see what's wrong with the second example? The word "boss" is still there, and that's still an external factor. If you removed all the external factors completely, you will start becoming more accountable for your actions. That's exactly what you should do.

You can change the example above to the following:

- You have spent many years in your job but you're still not promoted. Why?

- Because I am not doing my job well. Why?

- Because I do not feel like it. Why?

- Because I feel stressed at work. Why?

- Because there are too many things to do. Why?

- Because I wasn't able to finish some of them yesterday. Why?

- Because I showed up late. Why?

- Because I woke up late. Why?

- Because I slept late.

Now, there's your habit: Sleeping late and getting up late. Doing these things repeatedly causes stress in your work. List these habits down and name your list Life Habits, because these have impact on your life without you knowing it.

By now, you have your Primary Habits, Secondary Habits, and Life Habits lists. You can proceed to the next step to see how you can break these habits down and how you are going to change them.

Chapter 5

8 Elements of a Habit Stacking Routine

Element #1: Each habit takes less than five minutes to complete

Each habit within your habit-stacking routine takes less than five minutes to complete. This means each task is simple and doesn't require a major time commitment, making it easy to finish and move on to the next habit.

A great example of a quick one-minute habit is collecting all your loose change and adding it to a change jar, or sending a text message to a friend that you haven't connected with in a while

Element #2: It's a complete habit

A complete habit is an action that cannot be built upon. For example, exercising is a habit that can be built upon. Exercises change, increase or decrease, and develop over time. This is not the point of a habit within habit stacking. Each habit is a full action completed in a short amount of time— like making your bed. It is basically the same action every day and doesn't vary much in the time it takes to complete.

Element #3: It improves your life

Habit stacking is done with the purpose of improving your life. The positive changes that come along with habit stacking are reflected specifically in one of seven areas: productivity, relationships, finances, organization, spirituality/ mental well-being, health/ physical fitness and leisure.

Element #4: It's simple to complete

Since each habit takes less than five minutes to complete, it's natural that none of the habits are complicated or rigorous. The simplicity of each habit allows you to complete it and move on to the next, sticking to the routine and making a lot of positive changes quickly and efficiently.

Each habit takes only a few small steps to complete. One example is unsubscribing from a retail email newsletter. You can do this by taking a few simple actions that take only a few seconds each.

Element #5: It takes less than 30 minutes

Your complete habit stacking routine should take up just 15 to 30 minutes when you string all of the quick actions together. If you're new to habit stacking, start by focusing on habits that add up to around 15 minutes of your day. This will help you avoid being overwhelmed and ensure you complete all of your habits.

With a 15-minute routine, it's possible for you to complete anywhere from three to thirty small changes. Even if you add new habits, it's important to keep your routine to less than 30 minutes. If you create a routine lasting longer than 30 minutes, there's a chance it will take too much of your time, making it difficult to complete your list.

Element #6: It Follows a logical process

Your habit stacking routine should flow like a well-oiled machine. You complete each action, moving from room to room quickly and consistently. If you take breaks in between actions, you are wasting both time and energy. This could prevent you completing the entire routine.

The whole process should be like a production line, with constant action until all the habits are complete. Every time you complete the routine, it will get easier and become more habitual, resulting in many positive life changes over the course of the next few weeks or months.

Element #7: It follows a checklist

Habit stacking isn't meant to be a guessing game, or to be improvised on a day-to-day basis. It should be a set of actions done the same way, in the same order, each day. The best way to make sure this happens is to have the habits written down in a checklist. That way, you always know which task comes next and feel a sense of accomplishment as you get through each item on your list. Checklists do much more than keep people organized; they also increase productivity.

Element #8: It fits your life

It's important to leverage your day in habit stacking. Take advantage of your location and the time of day when it comes to your habits. Energy is usually at its peak during the first part of your day, which means you should be completing habits that inspire or excite you about the day ahead.

A great example is sending an inspirational quote or story to a loved one. It takes energy to find such a piece of content and decide who to send it to, but this habit is highly rewarding and will help you kick off your day feeling great and ready to tackle all the following habits you have in your routine.

Chapter 6

Useful Life Habits

Really, all of the habits in this book should hopefully be useful to you in some way. This section will include more such habits that you can implement in your everyday life. They are simple to use, they're effective, and they can help you further develop your intellectual abilities.

Habit #20

Ask for Help When You Need it

Running into a difficult challenge happens to everyone. Just because you don't know how to do something doesn't mean you'll never figure it out. When this happens, it's a good idea to find someone who knows more about the topic and who can help you learn. You may be uncomfortable seeking help, but if you aren't making any progress or if you're falling behind on something important that you want or need to learn, sometimes there is no better option. The good thing is there is usually someone more than willing to help if you look around.

It's common to need help at some point, and it really makes a difference to get that help instead of trying to force yourself over and over to come up with a solution. Especially if you are getting no results by doing this. If you are studying or learning a difficult topic, you may be surprised at just how many people need tutors and extra help.

As an example, I made a mistake when I was a freshman in high school. Algebra was the hardest thing in the world for me, but I refused to get help. I'd spend frustrating hours studying at night, still with a poor understanding. Eventually after months of hanging on by a thread, I decided to get help. Luckily, my teacher offered to tutor me in the mornings. I went from a frustrated C/D student with horrible understanding, to a comfortable A-/ B+ student with a very good understanding after two months of tutoring. I don't think I could have gotten caught up without the extra help. An important thing I want to note is that to this day I consider myself pretty strong in algebra. I had to work so hard to learn it (with the help of a great teacher) that even after years of not using it I can still recall the main principles.

How to apply this habit

If you feel lost:

- Ask a teacher, mentor, a friend, or someone

knowledgeable for help

- Seek out a study group, or start one of your own
- Find a helpful forum online where you can ask questions by Googling [Problem topic area + "forum"]

Habit #21

Form Analogies

Analogies are great for explaining concepts to other people, and also helpful for solidifying your own understanding of a topic. As you know, an analogy usually compares what you're trying to learn with something else that you already know. It's like a bridge that builds a path toward a better understanding. This is one of the fastest ways you can form new connections and begin to clearly understand a topic.

With an analogy, something that is complex can be made simple and easy to understand – this is very powerful. A concept that is shapeless and confusing can suddenly take shape and make perfect sense with the right analogy. Analogies are about taking what is commonly known and bringing clarity to a topic that you don't quite understand yet. They are great both for teaching and learning new concepts and ideas.

As an example, in the movie "Forrest Gump", Forrest says "Life is like a box of chocolates. You never know what you're going to get." This is actually a pretty good example of an analogy, because Forrest uses something concrete and easily understood, a box of chocolates, to explain something more abstract and not always easily understood, life. Of course, life is much more complex than just a box of chocolates. But the point of an analogy isn't to perfectly explain something complex, it's to help foster understanding in a practical way.

How to apply this habit

- Come up with some analogies that apply in your day to day life – what is a good analogy for what you do at work? What is a good analogy for a hobby that you invest a lot of time into? Perhaps you can use these analogies to quickly explain what you do to others

- Compare concepts that you don't fully understand with other systems that you're more familiar with

- Learn broadly about how different systems work so you have more analogies in mind to quickly learn new things (i.e., mechanics, anatomy and physiology, evolution, etc.)

Habit #22

Write Down Your Thoughts (or Record Them)

Getting your thoughts down into words on paper makes you break them down and forces you to clarify exactly what you think, and why you think it. It's a challenge. When writing, it's usually a good idea to put down reasons why you feel or think the way you do. This causes you to actively think about the situation, consider alternative viewpoints, and evaluate specifically how you came to your conclusions.

Writing is a good exercise for your memory, because you'll often want to think back on experiences you've had that support your argument or your thoughts on something. The more events you can recall from memory that support a point, the more likely you are to feel strongly that you have good reason to believe what you do. If you find weak support in your memories, you may decide it's better to question your thinking, and perhaps you've been too quick to take a position on an issue.

Another useful part about writing is that by maintaining a record of your thoughts, you can always look back on them later. In the future you'll be able to look back on your thoughts and evaluate if you've learned something new that invalidates your old thoughts. Or perhaps you will have learned something new that further supports what you used to think. Another possibility is that you've moved on and found issues that are of greater importance than the ones you used to worry about.

I've kept logs occasionally of some of my thoughts throughout my life. It's interesting to look back and see what kinds of things were important to me at different points in life. Logging my thoughts and experiences has helped me to better evaluate where I've been and where I want to be in the future.

How to apply this habit

- Record your progress on an important goal in your life

- Record a great learning experience that you had

- Write about a mistake you made and what you learned from it

- Write down your thoughts on a book you read and what you learned

- As you record your thoughts, look for supporting memories or facts for why you hold your conclusions and write them down as well

Habit #23

Organize Your Notes

If you have notes (or files of them) for work that are important for you to know and understand, then organizing them physically can also help you organize them mentally. You may feel comfortable having all of your notes available to you, but this alone isn't enough for them to be useful. To really understand them, the notes have to be organized. You'll probably want to have them neatly filed or in a notebook or binder. But beyond that, the information needs to be arranged in a way that makes it more likely for you to understand and remember. Intelligence isn't just about knowing more facts. It's also about understanding how things connect, how they're organized, and how they work.

If you have trouble understanding something, you might make a mind map, an outline, a flow chart, or a Venn diagram to further break it down into simple steps that really make sense. (If you're not familiar with these, informative links are provided at the end of this section.) You may even create a dictionary of terms for yourself if you find that certain concepts are giving you a lot of problems with comprehending your notes.

When I have trouble understanding a field or a topic, I like to mind map it out to see how everything interrelates and interconnects. Of course, your preference for organizing your notes really depends on your expertise level, how your mind works, and your area of study. Perhaps for your notes, a flow chart or a Venn diagram makes more sense than a mind map. This is something you need to consider.

How to apply this habit

- Use a notebook, Evernote, or another program, to organize files and delete or put into a junk folder items that are no longer important
- Make an outline
- Make a mind map
- Make a flow chart
- Make a Venn diagram
- Create a dictionary of terms (where you define all important concepts)

Habit #24

Define Your Top Goal for the Day

Smart people get things done, and I find this to be one of the simplest and most useful habits to help focus and get things done. Sure, you can write down your #2 and #3 goals, but usually my #1 goal dictates the whole tone of a day. My #2 and #3 and so forth goals will often come about naturally as things I need to do to support my #1 goal for the day.

A clear directed focus is an important part of being smart. A great way to do that is to know exactly what you want to accomplish the next day, especially the biggest priority. Intelligent people avoid wasting time in the morning. They already know beforehand what the most important thing they need to do is. It's easy to burn up time doing things that are not so important when we don't have some kind of plan. This is why it's important to at least know your top goal for the day every day. It's a good idea either to make a note of this the night before, or at least to get up early in the morning to make sure you know your top priority.

This smart habit comes from personal experience. When I don't have my goal for the day clearly laid out, I find that I may not get started on anything important until later in the day. If I don't have a plan, the first few hours of my day will tend to go toward things that may be easier, but not especially important. I make sure to always follow this habit now, because I know it really helps.

How to apply this habit

- Before you go to bed, get a notecard and write down your #1 priority for the next day that you absolutely want to accomplish – consider an item that if you were to accomplish it, would bring you closer to meeting your biggest goals

- If you think of a few tasks that support that goal, you can write those down as well

- Make sure to put 100% of your focus on your top priority until you are finished

Habit #25

Think Ahead and Have Backup Plans

Many of us might like to plan something and then stick to that plan. Having a plan often helps as opposed to having no idea how you want to do something. However, plans can change, sometimes in ways you didn't expect. Not only this, but so many things happen in the course of the day that it's not realistic to try to plan ahead for absolutely everything.

As a result of plans changing frequently, and being unable to plan for everything, it's a smart habit to regularly be thinking ahead. This is a good way to avoid auto-piloting and keeping your mind active. If you're driving, you may think "What's next?" First I'm dropping off the kids at daycare. Then I'm going to stop at the coffee shop for breakfast. Then I'll going to work but I have to take a different street because the one I usually take is shut off. As simple as this all seems, if you're not thinking ahead it's easy to waste time or make a costly mistake.

Thinking about what's next is a very useful habit. It can involve memory, as in the example above the driver remembers that there is construction and he should take a different way to work. It obviously involves planning skills, and you may have to predict if you do one action, what will happen next. You may evaluate if there are better alternatives. This can involve questioning and analyzing possibilities. This is a useful habit because you can save time and avoid problems.

How to apply this habit

- When driving, ask yourself how you can best get to your destination efficiently

- When doing your work, ask yourself what you need to do after you finish your current project

- For important events, try to come up with at least one backup plan that you can implement if everything doesn't work out exactly as you expected

Habit #26

Make Learning Fun, Interesting, and Relevant

Sometimes you have to learn something because it's

important for school, work, or some other important need, and you don't have much of a choice. In that case, you need to find a way to make it fun and interesting. Smart people know how to learn even when they're not in the mood. Usually, they will be happy to learn because smart people tend to be quite curious, but no one is always in the mood to learn everything.

It's important to do this because if your brain interprets what you're learning as dry and boring, then you're going to have to repeat the material to yourself over and over just to learn it because your brain is telling you 'this doesn't really matter'. When you find a way to make learning fun, engaging, and relevant to your life, it will come much easier. You'll begin to absorb the material in a way you otherwise wouldn't.

One thing I'll do is look hard to determine a way that what I'm learning is relevant to me personally, or figuring out a scenario when I might need to use it. This can be a stretch, especially for more abstract topics or topics that involve past time periods. One thing that keeps me going is that I don't like to be seen as ignorant. This can only take me so far though. If the pressure is high to learn something I feel is boring, I may try to turn learning the material into a fun challenge of some kind.

How to apply this habit

- Practice making up funny stories out of what you're learning

- Practice finding personal relevancy in what you learn

- Practice dramatizing what you learn, as if it were a Hollywood movie

- For stories or history, pretend that you are the main character – this helps make it matter and become emotionally vivid

Habit #27

Apply What You Read or Learn

You should realize that the best way to truly learn something is to try it for yourself. It's important to make sure that when a topic is important to you that you don't get too hung up on reading or analyzing endlessly. Reading and analyzing are good ways of learning and developing your thinking, but at some point the best thing you can do is put what you know to use.

It's common for people to worry about making a mistake, and this is a real possibility in anything we do. When the possible mistakes are costlier, perhaps it's a good idea to read more and analyze more. But when the possible mistakes are not likely to cost you much, it's better to read less, analyze less, and do something instead. You can learn a lot from putting to use what you've learned in books and through thinking and planning. Often times things won't go like you planned, or you'll make mistakes you didn't expect to make. And the best thing you can do is learn from those mistakes.

If you've been reading about gardening for a while, you might want to take the plunge and buy some seeds or small plants and get them in the ground already. If you've been reading about swimming technique but you don't know how to swim, you could be better off signing up for lessons from a good instructor. Also, if you've visited art museums to get a good idea of how to make a painting, you might want to pick up a brush already and start somewhere.

The problem we have sometimes is that we get stuck in a rut of reading and analyzing instead of acting and doing. Feel free to read and analyze, just make an effort to catch yourself when all you're doing is building up fear that you'll make a mistake instead of taking the plunge and seeing what you can actually do.

How to apply this habit

- While reading or learning something new, ask yourself frequently how the material applies to your life and how you can adapt the information for your specific needs

- If you get stuck in a rut of analyzing the same possibilities over and over, or if you find yourself worrying more about what can go wrong than about how to make progress, you should consider pushing through and taking action – Of course, analysis makes sense when the risks are too high to jump in

- If you have a teacher that doesn't clearly state the practical use of what they teach, then go ahead and ask

From Here, Where Do You Go?

If Plan – Do – Check – Act is too much to worry about, then just work on your smart habits as you have time. The important part is to make sure you are challenging your mind. The common denominator in all of the habits in this book is that they are meant to challenge you in some way. You don't want to get frustrated with too much challenge, and you don't want to do things that are too easy for you. It's important to find the right balance. Those are the best smart habits. You may even discover some of your own smart habits that you can use, and that's great too.

I've observed these habits in some of the smartest people I've known, and some I've discovered for myself. The ones I discovered myself were often by finding that I used bad habits that weren't working for me or someone pointed out that I had a bad habit. I don't claim to be perfect and always follow every habit listed. It's an ongoing effort, but I believe they are very worthwhile and I will continue to make efforts to implement them in my life. The best part of course is that these are habits anyone can get started with right away.

I'd like to add one last piece of advice before I leave you to get started. As I've pointed out, I learned about many smart habits through observation. If there was a time I realized I had done something foolish, I would simply stop and ask myself what I could have done better. If I noticed that someone I considered smart had a specific habit that got them results, I paid attention to that. Sometimes I would even ask what they were thinking or how they came to a solution to a problem. You may be surprised at what you can learn simply through observation and asking questions.

Through my observations and questions, I've only come to believe more strongly that what separates the very smart from everyone else is that they've learned what kind of habits get the best results. They tend to be the habits that challenge the mind and that involve learning and striving to understand more and more. After identifying those habits, they've committed themselves to taking action and using them regularly. The habits you need to get started are in this book. To improve your abilities and get results in your life you will have to put them into action.

Chapter 7

What do Successful People Avoid?

This book has spent a fair amount of time talking about what successful people do to get where they are and achieve great things, but there's something else that's equally important to discuss on this topic. That is what successful people avoid and reject.

What Successful People Avoid

People who are successful live their lives with purpose, truth, and great habits. The lives they lead don't appear out of thin air or because they're lucky, but because they make conscious choices to do what is healthy and productive. We've talked plenty about what the great thinkers and inventors of our world do, but what don't they do?

They Avoid Defining Greatness with Wealth:

The majority of successful people use inner peace, what they contribute to the world, and happiness, with their ultimate success, instead of how much money they make. Sure, not having to worry about money does help with opportunities and stress relief, but if you can't be happy without it, chances are you won't be happy once you do have it.

They Avoid having no Purpose:

Successful people know what they want in both the short and long term, but they also know what they need to do during each and every day to get closer to success and wellbeing. They also know that how they act and what they do during the first hour of waking will control how the rest of their day goes.

They Avoid Trying to be Perfect:

People who are truly successful aim for progress instead of some illusory vision of perfection. The problem with trying to be perfect is that you can easily become obsessed with picking out imperfections that need fixing. This often stunts growth and progress because you get so discouraged that you don't want to continue, or you get so distracted by trying to fix "problems" that you end up with an unfinished project. Once you realize that it isn't about making one goal completely perfect, but what you can learn along the way, you can constantly improve while leading a life of achievements and success.

They Avoid Negative Influences:

Being around people who make excuses, procrastinate, and complain will eventually have a bad effect on you and your success and dreams. Successful people know that it's important to have other success-minded folks in their midst who can challenge them, push them to achieve, and inspire them to be their best selves.

They Avoid thinking about the Negative:

We already discussed the importance of positivity in chapter three, but it's worth revisiting for this point. A truly successful person doesn't allow themselves to dwell on or get caught up in the negative points of life. When they reach a difficult situation, they will immediately start looking for positives to the situation and tell themselves that they can do it. They will also mentally review instances from their past that prove they can handle challenges. Instead of thinking about what could possibly go wrong, they see this as a waste of energy and instead focus on how they can succeed and learn lessons along the way.

They never Dwell on Mistakes or Failures:

People who are successful accept that mistakes and failures just come along with the territory of learning and growing. Any bumps along the path can be extra fuel for success in the future and opportunities to find out more about themselves. Even when things don't pan out exactly as they had hoped or planned for, they don't let this stop them.

They don't Focus too much on Problems:

When you think about the challenges and problems in front of you, it makes you feel stressed out and eve blocks you from seeing solutions or new ways to approach the situation. This then fuels a negative cycle and leads to more stress and, as a result, difficulties. But thinking about the actions you can take right now to improve the situation is a way to counteract this negative cycle. They are aware that getting caught up on problems and complaining about them will only intensify the bad, so they commit to being solution oriented instead.

They Avoid Worrying about Others' Judgment:

People who are truly successful will never decide how much they are worth based on what other people think about them, because they have already decided for themselves what their value is. Thus, they don't require validation from the people around them. They know that people have their own opinions, but it doesn't necessarily mean it's true or even that it has to affect you.

They Avoid Excuse-Making:

People who are successful are also highly proactive, meaning that they know how to get their goals achieved. They know that forces outside of them might interrupt their plans, but they know that only they can control the attitude they have in response to this. It's impossible to control all circumstances in life, but you can control the way you react and, as a result of this, your success.

They Avoid Being Jealous over Others' Success:

Those who succeed already know that there is no shortage of success out there and that another person winning does not take away from their personal worth or value. When they see others succeed and win, they're happy for them, not threatened or jealous. Another person's victory is a chance to learn something and become even more inspired to reach your own goals in life.

They Avoid Taking Life for Granted:

A successful person knows that they should be grateful instead of taking life for granted. This means you should appreciate yourself, the lessons you learn in life, a chance to be alive, and the support of your friends and family. Never forget to appreciate what you have while you have it.

Successful People Don't Miss out on Fun:

A successful person knows that there is little value in achievements if you don't make time to enjoy them. What is the real point in trying hard to succeed if you only end up frustrated and exhausted? You need to know how to have fun and relax if you're going to have a good life. Take breaks to recharge when you need to so you can enjoy savoring your achievements even more and get to thinking up your next big goal!

They Avoid Being Unhealthy:

When you are healthy, you are also energetic, full of life, and free to do whatever you please. If you want to be successful, you need to avoid unhealthy actions, behaviors, habits, and influences. Otherwise you will never rise to your fullest potential. Take an honest look at your habits and find out what you need to work on improving when it comes to your health.

They Avoid Setting Vague Goals:

A successful person always sets specific, clear, and measurable plans and goals. Being aware of precisely what you are hoping to achieve will keep you fueled and motivated to reach your goals. Coming up with a clear and unclouded action plan will keep your mind sharp and focused and allow you to approach your goals free of extra anxiety.

They Avoid Being Indecisive:

People who are truly successful make a decision about what they want to achieve, and then they go for it. As soon as a decision is made, they don't waste time wondering whether it was the right one and regretting it. They take responsibility for the choice. This is a habit that helps you build up your confidence because you prove to yourself that the choices you make can work and that you can do what you set your mind to. Being indecisive is bad for your self-esteem because eventually, you find out that you can't trust yourself.

They Avoid playing the Victim:

Any time they get affected by the bad choices of anther, successful people immediately process their bad feelings or emotions and allow themselves to let go and forgive. This way they minimize the negative results from that person. Instead of blaming their problems on others, they realize that their own happiness is their responsibility and no one else's, and therefore never play the victim role.

They Avoid Regret:

A successful person realizes that they can never change the past and that dwelling on it is not only pointless but extremely harmful. They would rather seize the day and live fully from where they are instead of trying to analyze what has already happened. You deserve a successful future, so focus on the now to get there. Chance is a natural part of this experience, so instead of getting frustrated at chances, learn how to shift along with the changes and stay motivated along the way.

Ultimately, to be a truly successful person who achieves great things, you need to stay open to always learning. A successful person isn't afraid to ask for advice or seek guidance from coaches or mentors. They are constantly learning and open to improving themselves. They never end their day without thinking about the good things that happened. If you want to be one of the successful ones, make these habits part of your life now.

Chapter 8

Creating Big Goals for Success

In the beginning of this book, we cautioned against getting too caught up in big goals when you are planning out your future. Try for smaller ones at first. But what happens when you have established these habits for success and achieved the small goals you've set before yourself. What next? At this stage, learning how to aim higher is essential for growing. Aiming high involves setting ambitious and huge goals and staying focused enough to accomplish them. This depends on the notion that you are the only barrier between yourself and success.

How to find what you want:

What have you always wanted? For some, this is an easy and obvious question, but for others it isn't quite so simple. If you aren't sure how to answer this question, do a simple exercise first. Take a piece of paper and pen and write the question at the top. Then spend some time doing a free writing session where you explore this question. If the answer doesn't immediately appear, don't worry. Just keep writing until it does. You will know when you've finally broken through and found the answer to what you've always wanted to do. This is what your goals should be based on.

If you believe you can't, you're correct:

If you already believe that you're incapable of achieving something, you'll be correct about that. If, on the other hand, you're determined to find a way to accomplish what you want to achieve, you will find a way. Every department and operation of your business or project should involve big goals for the long term. We've talked a bit about the importance of daily habits, but how else should your goals be framed?

- Monthly Goals: When you get up each day and complete the tasks you've decided to achieve, what is it that keeps you going? You should have a single goal you're aiming for each and every month that you can refer back to and keep yourself on track with. This can be marked on your calendar or simply posted on your wall as a reminder.

- Yearly Goals: Next, we have yearly goals. What do you want to have achieved by this time next year? Perhaps you are dreaming of being in shape and losing weight, or of having your foot in the door at your dream job. Maybe you dream of starting at a local university. Think about what you truly want and make it your year-long plan.

If you don't bother to think big, you are missing out on chances to become more productive, efficient, and successful. So, when you're crafting your yearly goals or five-year plan, reach as high as you possibly can. The great inventors of the world weren't held back by thoughts of their dreams being impossible, instead they believed it could happen and achieved it.

Breaking down mental barriers:

You may automatically hear your inner-voice tell you your goals are too big when you are trying to craft them, but the trick is to find goals, at first, that seem only slightly "too big." Once you achieve these, you will have the confidence you need to keep crafting larger and larger goals. Then when you aim huge, even if you don't reach your ultimate goal, you will still have achieved something amazing.

Never sell yourself short or create unnecessary mental barriers by telling yourself your dreams aren't possible. What is the point of aiming for something mediocre when you feel passionate about something bigger? Always remember to see barriers, obstacles, and mistakes along the way as hidden lessons you can use as ammo to do better and succeed next time. Follow all of this and you will be one of the great success stories in no time!

Chapter 9

Habits That Lead to Success

If certain habits help to maintain a beautiful relationship with the person we love, most certainly they can help you reach success in our professional life as well.

You need to have the right set of habits if you want to enjoy success because not any habit will bring such fruitful results. In fact, most successful people have developed habits that helped them on their journey towards success, while also allowing them to maintain this status and enjoy a fulfilling life. Most certainly you are curious to find out what these habits are, so take a look at the following list and see what you can do to improve your life and reach success faster.

Habit #28

Be the best version of you

If you want to make it and face the harsh competition that exists on the market today, the only way to do so is by being a few steps ahead of your clients and even your boss. Be the best person you can be and look for ways that will make you the first in every situation.

How to do this? Each time you are requested to do something, to perform a certain task, try to think ahead and foresee what other tasks and requests will follow next. Thus, you will be able to perform these tasks before they are even asked, proving that you are not only result-oriented and efficient, but you also know what you are doing and you're ambitious when it comes to your work and personal performance.

Habit #29

Be organized

It is hard to achieve anything if you are not properly organized. Every successful person has a clear image of how a day should look like, the organization in his or her mind being highly visible in the environment where such a person will work. It's been said that behind an organized desk you will find an organized mind. The more organized and neat you are, the faster you will achieve the goals you have set for the day. Not everybody gets born with an organized mind, but this is a skill that can be learned and perfected.

Habit #30

Always show respect

You should always be a person that shows respect to the people around you, by being careful of what you speak and what you do. Being respectful can get you a long way, your performances and results being more noticeable if you are known as a respectful person. Showing disrespect will not only keep you away from reaching success but may even get you unemployed.

Habit #31

Show an increased resistance

Successful people never cave in, no matter what, always finding the strength to bounce back and start all over if necessary. The road towards success is not an easy one, so you should prepare to face many challenges that may come your way. Not managing to get things done as you would like to or even facing failure should not bring you down. You have to be aware that life will bring you many other opportunities, so you have to be up and ready to spot them as they arrive, instead of letting them pass by.

Habit #32

Stop postponing things

Stop waiting for the perfect moment or finding various reasons that will keep you from doing what you know you need to do. Each time you postpone something, you actually lose precious time. So act now! Do it because no one had perfect training, knowledge, or experience when starting out. Just be flexible and ready to change the plan as you go, in case adjustments are needed to make things flow easier and more efficiently.

Habit #33

Always hold on to your sense of humour

This doesn't mean that you will start taking things lightly, your job still being a serious and important part of your life. Having a sense of humor and a bit of laughter now and then will help you keep stress at bay, which means you will be able to tackle even the toughest of challenges. Most people enjoy the company of someone that has a good sense of humor, because such persons will help them unwind and feel better as well.

Habit #34

Don't be scared to take risks

Risks are part of life and you should not be afraid to take a leap from time to time, even if you are not sure what the outcome will be. Every successful person today has taken several risks on their path towards success because they understood that this is the only way to get where they want to be. Sometimes, by doing so, they had to face disappointment, which is also a normal thing when searching for success. But, they also encountered real rewards, which were generated by their courage to take risks when the situation required it.

Habit #35

Do not forget about praises

Whether it is about praising your co-workers, team members, or even yourself, praises should be an important ingredient in your recipe for reaching success. You see, people will work harder and do their best if they see that their efforts and dedication are noticed. So, instead of believing that praising will make them rest on their laurels, do have in mind that such encouragements and acknowledgments of their work and results are necessary to establish good work relationships and a proactive working environment.

Habit #36

Be up to date with technology

Every successful person will look for new ways that will make work processes more efficient, cutting down the spend time and resources. So, make sure you are aware of the latest breakthroughs in technology, especially those that fit in your line of business and activity and see how they can improve what you are doing. If you want to stay ahead of everyone, you will need all the help you can get.

Chapter 10

Good Habits to Improve Your Health

A healthy life is a symbol of a better standard of living. Everyone in today's community is consciously aware of making their health at its best. There is no guarantee of having a healthier and sound body. There can be incidents in our lives which affect our health and daily lives in a variety of ways, such as environment, territories, sound and air pollution, global warming, personal psychological disorders and lack of good personal care. Besides these unwanted elements, one can overcome the redundancy in one's health by adopting some healthier activities and hobbies. These hobbies can lessen the effect of these factors. Below is a list of healthy habits that you can practice to improve your health.

Habit #37

Have a good breakfast every morning

Vitamins and proteins are essential for maintaining a healthy body. Research has reported that people who have a healthy breakfast are likely to attain the right quantity of proteins and vitamins. Even so, you need to avoid meals high in fat and cholesterol. Cholesterol makes your body bulky and messy while fatty meals can make your day dull; the combination of these effects is unbearable by any profession or business body. It is, therefore, important to take juices and vegetables as they are the best resources of vitamins and proteins. Moreover, eggs and yogurt provide energy to a working body.

Habit #38

Add eggs and fatty acids to your diet

Fishes such as herring, sardines, lake trout and albacore tuna are not only tasty but also medicinal. Eating seafood to boost your health and help you fight many unknown diseases, it also helps us to maintain our pulse rate and metabolism. AHA (American Heart Association) recommends eating fish twice a week. Add eggs and foods such as canola oil, soybean, tofu and flaxseed to your diet. Omega-3, a type of fatty acid found in fish, is used to soothe overactive immune system and can be taken in small quantity to boost your immunity. Moreover, it is employed in the treatment of asthma, eczema, and allergies.

Habit #39

Get adequate sleep

Ideally, we would be spending nearly one-third of our entire lives asleep, and we know that sleep is extremely important to our health and happiness. It has such an influence on our lives, for better or worse, so it makes sense that we should invest in better sleep. How much is your health and happiness worth to you? How much of an effect is sleep or lack of good sleep has in your life?

Those who do not sleep enough hours throughout the night typically experiences increased hunger levels. Despite the fact that there is not much higher energy expenditure throughout the day, your body will still feel hunger, causing you to want to consume more calories.

Since excess calories directly correlate with weight gain, this makes for a very challenging situation for someone attempting to maintain their body weight.

Habit #40

Take a walk every day

Taking a walk in the morning makes you feel happy, healthier and joyful. Fresh air in our lungs regulates throughout the whole body and makes our respiratory system productive and easier. Don't think to become a hero from in one day. Adopting this habit shall take time.

Habit #41

Explore social connections

Watching movies with friends on the weekend or playing chess with your father boosts your social relationships. Social satisfaction provides a state of accomplishment and makes you a happy person.

Habit #42

Exercise to regulate blood flow

Exercise is inevitable in maintaining good health; this helps control weight, maintain healthy joints and muscles. According to National Cancer Center, exercise is essential to escape premature death. Exercise is not just pulling up heavy weights; it is a way to stretch our body and to redefine it to the extent that we can.

Habit #43

Take care of your skin

Skin is the most important part of our body, and it deserves our attention. Wash your face with a good cleanser twice a day and use soothing lotions. Avoid direct overexposure to the sun and instead, use hats and handkerchief when sitting or walking in the sun.

Habit #44

Maintain Dental hygiene

The bacteria produced by teeth after eating is said it gets into our blood. Research shows that these bacteria are associated with inflammation, which blocks blood vessels and results in heart diseases. Brushing and flossing our teeth can prevent various diseases such as gum diseases, like dementia and arthritis. And a useful way to resist cavities.

Habit #45

Taking tea

Tea is a Universal meditation. Many people around the world take tea, as it is said to heal the body and protect it from various diseases. Tea is also said to have a significant impact on cancer. Therefore, it is essential to include tea in your breakfast. It is also helpful as it keeps you awake at night when in an emergency or when having work burden.

Chapter 11

How Good Habits Can Change Your Life?

Good habits, as we've discussed earlier, will help you on your way to success. But, there are many more ways in which it will completely change your life and you. Here is a small list of five things that are guaranteed to happen to you once you've cultivated the habits and routines mentioned in the book.

Confidence

Since you've been working towards becoming successful all this time, you will find that achievement after achievement will boost your confidence. At the same time, careful planning and calculated risks will ensure you approach your work with cautiousness. This will keep you from getting arrogant. Arrogance, believe me, is the last thing you need.

Help you avoid stress

When you make good habits a routine, it acts as an

autopilot, steering you in the right direction. You will find yourself dealing with reduced levels of stress. Having cultivated a habit of planning your day in advance ensures that you are always in control of the situation. It pays to always be on top of the situation, that way you control speed and direction of things. Habits like exercising each day, starting your day off with a glass of lemon juice and taking time out to relax will keep stress away from you.

Trust and respect

Following a routine will make you a more reliable person and reliability is a characteristic that is appreciated in all aspects of life. If you cultivate good habits, like the habit of always reaching on time, you are likely to be respected for it. When a client is faced with a multitude of options to employ from, the goodwill and reliability attached to your name will increase your chances of landing the job. Following a routine means that you are in control of your life, this leaves you with mind space to deal with other problems. When you enable yourself to calmly inspect problems and provide solutions, you will find people wanting to work with you.

Efficiency

Practice makes one perfect, routine is daily practice, the best kind there is! Good habits like reading daily, planning your day, focusing will equip you with all you need to be a highly efficient employee. Get more done in less time. You can do that only if you master your primary skills and have a well-planned approach towards tackling your job. Don't put in unnecessary effort. They say "lazy people are the smartest, they always find a shortcut to finishing their work" you needn't be lazy but you can be smart.

Improvement in health

Daily exercise obviously helps you improve your health. But remember, we have not just cultivated good habits, we've made the replace the bad ones. Exercise on top of having cut down on smoking and drinking will see you becoming healthy as a horse in no time. Waking up early every day is another habit that improves health. It allows us to have our meals earlier than we would have otherwise had. In fact, fixed times for meals is another habit worth having. However, waking up early doesn't mean you sacrifice your sleep.

I've listed down just a few of the results you can expect. Good habits take you a long way, and you will find many unexpected outcomes. Unexpected and positive. That is, actually, the biggest advantage of a healthy routine. It brings positivity into your life. Positivity is in the mind, so when the mind is calm, work gets sorted faster. You will find yourself being able to deal with unexpected problems at work quite easily. If you have a short temper, these good habits might even take care of that.

Chapter 12

Finding Time to Relax

Work, rest and play all have an equal part in how much you enjoy your life. If all your life has in it is work, then you become dull. If you only relax and don't want to work, you become lazy. Therefore, there has to be balance of these three elements. Work, Rest and Play need to be a part of your everyday life because when the balance is thrown out, you veer toward stress on the one hand and apathy on the other and neither of these are positive ways of looking at life. In this chapter, we deal with relaxation because if you want to be good at what you do, you need to have a certain amount of your life dedicated to having fun and relaxing.

Look at your existing habit list and decide where you could add a little relaxation and make it appropriate to your everyday life. For example, it may not be appropriate to have a lie down in the lunch hour at work, but it may be appropriate to take a crossword puzzle into the park at lunchtime. You need to decide what activities help you to relax and stimulate your mind at the same time. Some people enjoy video games because they feel that they allow them to switch off the real world for a moment. Some people enjoy doing word puzzles or increasing their vocabulary. One thing that we know is that positive habits work, while introducing negative ones isn't helpful. Whatever you choose to incorporate into your day that helps you to relax should be positively beneficial.

Sitting down to enjoy a sandwich instead of eating on the go can help you to relax. Try to look at your habit list and add things that can turn into habits that are easy to incorporate and that will become part of your everyday life and will help you to get the relaxation you deserve.

Chapter 13

Productivity at Work

Chances are that you sometimes feel overwhelmed by the amount of work that you have. Most people do and that's normal but what they don't know is that by introducing small habits, they can actually be more productive and worry less. What you need to look at is the habits that make your workload heavy and some of them will be negative habits that hinder your progress. For example, do you allow yourself to be interrupted too often? Do you jump from one job into another or try to multi-task? Did you know that scientists recommend that concentrating on one task at a time means that you finish it quicker? The mind was not made to multi task and when you do that, you actually take more time to finish all the tasks at hand.

The most energetic time of day – as far as logic and thought processes go – is first thing in the morning and directly after a light lunch. I say a light lunch because although some people do have a full meal at lunchtime, a heavy meal may make you lethargic and tired, rather than energized. Thus, if you have jobs that need to be done, these should be prioritized. This also helps you to see when you need less interaction with people so that your levels of concentration are greater. Triaging your work gives you great power over how much you get done.

There will be three categories:

- High priority – concentration needed
- Medium priority – Things you can do while talking to other colleagues
- Low Priority – Things that are quick to do and less important

Life within the workplace doesn't have to be stressful. Look at habits that you have and introduce new positive ones that relate to the workplace and that make your day much more productive and enjoyable. That way, your workload becomes lighter and you find the time to concentrate on those things that are important. It's all a question of your habitual approach to work and modifying it by adding new habits. When you do that, you change other people's attitudes too because they respond to who you show yourself to be and with the new habits, this will be a more positive you.

Chapter 14

Habits to Improve Your Finances

Of course, we all know that money is most important in today's world and it is most prudent that we use those habit-forming abilities of ours to create habits that will help us manage those finances of ours better, in an attempt to make sure that we are able to be as financially comfortable as we possibly can.

Let's take a look, then, at the best possible habits that we can inculcate to ensure that we have stellar control over those finances of ours.

Habit #46

Control impulse spending

We have learned early on that those habits begin with that 'impulse' out there, haven't we? Well, that impulse is certainly quite dominant when it comes to 'impulse spending'. The truth is, we all like to do things like eating out and shopping online, all of which constitute impulse spending, which can really burn a large hole into our savings account if we are not quite careful. So, make sure that you make a habit of not giving into those impulses for most of the times that they occur, because they will most certainly occur 'a lot'.

Habit #47

Set aside money for that emergency fund

You need to be constantly in the habit of saving money for that emergency fund in case of a problem that might crop up at any given instant in time. The truth is, you never quite know when anything might go wrong and you really need to make sure that whenever there is excess money in the bank, part of it goes towards that emergency fund of yours!

Habit #48

Eliminate those debts

Quite possibly the easiest way for you to find yourself in a financial conundrum would be to take on far more debt than you can possibly manage. You need to make sure that you work towards eliminating those debts that you might have accrued consistently, so that they are finally taken care of in the future, thanks to the habitual process of working on them in an attempt to clear them out.

Habit #49

Spend wisely

This does not mean that you should cut off all luxuries from your life. You should indulge yourself with the good things in life, but that doesn't mean that you go overboard and splurge on things that you don't really need. By only spending on what you need, you will find that you have more than what you want and are able to splurge 'occasionally' without feeling the 'hit' as far as your pocket is concerned.

Chapter 15

Daily Habits That Can Help You Increase Your Level of Self-Discipline

It is not just about developing or building self-discipline, it is also important to ensure that you sustain and increase your self-discipline by engaging in some daily activities that make you more disciplined. Here are some daily habits you could cultivate to improve your level of self-discipline.

Habit #50

Have an Attitude of Gratitude

Don't spend your whole life thinking of things you would have loved to have, which for one reason or the other have eluded you thus far. Having an attitude of gratitude teaches you to be thankful for what you have. Having an attitude of gratitude for the little you have can open the doors for the plenty you desire to flood into your life. This attitude of gratitude even when you obviously do not have enough helps you build your self-discipline.

Gratitude comes with a whole lot of benefits, from improving the state of your mental health to enhancing your emotional wellbeing. Most importantly, gratitude helps you detach from your state of lack and scarcity. Thinking about the things you desire which you have not been able to get will make it hard for you to attain the level of self-discipline you need to achieve your goals.

If you think it about it very well, if you don't have a gratitude attitude, then you must be tending to do the opposite: complaining about the few you have or not being satisfied with it. This surely leads you to a state of constant refusal to your current situation and can make you do one of the most terrible mistakes: dream about what you don't have and just stay there. Complaining about your current situation will make you reject open doors, even if they are in front of you. You cannot stay in an attitude of, "Why is this happening to me, Why me, If I had this or that, I never get what I what, It is not enough with what I have". Can you see how much energy you are wasting in that moment thinking that way? You're turning your entire current situation into bad energies out of the blue, and you remain with them, making you stop from thinking positively. You cannot do that. I've read once this, "If you are born poor it is not your fault, but if you die poor, it is your fault". You have all the necessary power to get what you want, but first you must be in harmony thanking for all what you currently have and what you, step by step, are getting. Once you are grateful, your mental state grows, opening the door to new opportunities.

Habit #51

Forgive

When it comes to forgiveness, you must learn to forgive both yourself and others to enable you to get ahead in life. Learning to forgive yourself when you err and others when they hurt you, helps build up your energy for success and makes you more disciplined. Whenever people hurt you, just forgive them and empty your mind of the load of hate and malice. Forgiving people who hurt you helps you release all negative energy that makes you lose your self-discipline. Please, you must get rid of the negative energy, because holding it will make you feel tired, discouraged, and angry all the time, plus it subtracts you the capability of thinking.

Habit #52

Meditate

Engaging in meditations helps put your mind at ease. It creates a type of spiritual atmosphere around you to help you grow and become a better you. Meditation sets the stage for you to attain a higher state of self-discipline by clearing the palette of your mind and putting you in the right mood to face the challenges of the day.

A simple meditation technique is to sit down on the floor with your legs folded in front of you, close your eyes, remove your mind from all worries, and focus on your breaths with your palms facing upwards. The time recommended for meditation is 15 minutes, if you are beginning. This has proven results due to the powering force you get by displacing all the negative energy and thoughts for nothing, preparing yourself to receive good energy and new ways to face things. This is an unconscious process. So, when you are starting to do this, perhaps you won't understand totally what it is all about, but once you have it as a good habit, you will find that it will help you cleanse your soul.

Habit #53

Set Active Goals for Each Day

Active goals are active because they can be seen. You make your goals active by putting them down on paper and placing them where they can be seen. Active goals help you build and increase your level of self-discipline because they give your life daily directions. This is when I talk about daily activities. There's no need to have an extreme objective or dream to set active goals; in fact, there are activities, such as washing the clothes, reading books, cooking, sleeping 8 hours a day, etc. that you will need to do every day. You can start with those home activities to increase your self-discipline.

You can have goals really important in your life that you want to accomplish, but you have to do everything that a successful person does in his daily routine. So, if you schedule these activities and set daily goals with the purpose of complying with them, you will be working on your self-discipline. This will help you eliminate procrastination.

Habit #54

Eat Right

When you eat the right foods, you help your body store more energy. When your diet is mostly composed of fats, carbohydrates and proteins, your body dissipates lots of energy processing such foods. When you eat more of fruits and veggies which require less energy to be processed, you will experience an energy boost that will help you pursue your goals with adequate level of self-discipline. Also, having the schedule of meals and with this I mean eating on time, will help you to have a healthy life when it comes to ingesting the right aliments in the right time. This way you will avoid having diseases or stomach problems, such as gastritis. Having these health problems will only take part of your time to recover and you will have to postpone the activities of your goals. It is preferable to prevent than to cure.

Get Enough Sleep

There is a direct link between sleep and self-discipline. Whether you give your body enough rest by getting adequate sleep or not goes a long way to determine your ability to stay focused on your goal to achieve self-discipline, and your general well-being. Make sure you get 6-8 hours of sleep no matter how busy you are. Avoid caffeinated drinks before bedtime. Doing this, will make you guarantee the good performance of the next day. Another thing to consider when it comes to sleeping is that insomnia time cannot be retrieved. It causes a permanent impact in your health and your general state. Medical researchers have proven that sleeping enough time every day will make you look younger and longevity increases. That is due to the time of rest you dedicate to your body that is reflected on your face and your activeness for the next day. Besides, getting enough sleep will help you release all the stress caused by work and very prompt activities.

Habit #55

Exercise Daily

Incorporating physical exercises into your daily routines helps you get rid of bad habits and adopt positive habits. If you really want to learn to discipline yourself, make certain physical exercises part of your morning routine. Most people give the excuse that they are too busy or have a lot of worries to get involved in physical exercises. Where such people get it wrong is that they forget they can improve their entire lives through physical exercises. Engaging in daily exercises helps you get rid of pains, anxiety, stress, and fatigue because when you exercise, your body releases hormones like endorphin and neurotransmitters such as serotonin and dopamine.

If you want to include to your life activities working out, whether to stay fit or just to collaborate with your health, you should be aware that having a good hygiene and getting enough hours to sleep will complement this habit. It is a terrible mistake to be working out and having eating disarrays, not sleeping the recommended 6-8 hours a day and not having the good hygiene. If you do this, you are simply working on your malaise. You have to take into account that several good habits complement each other and, when it comes to health, we cannot play. Always take care of yourself and look out your health. You can do easy exercises if you are starting, and as long as you continue, you can improve your workout routines.

Habit #56

Stay organized

Don't just wake up and start working on your goals for the day. Make sure you have your goals and daily tasks arranged in an orderly manner. Arranging your goals in an orderly manner helps you stay organized which is a good sign of self-discipline. Being organized goes beyond having a list of things to do, taking into account priorities. It also involves organizing all areas of your life such as your work table, your drawer, your kitchen cabinets, your wardrobe, your garage, your bedroom, and all other such spaces in your life.

Consider that you have several goals to accomplish and you have done some of your daily activities but you need to return home. There, you will finish the remaining activities for the day, but when you reach home, you find yourself in a disarrayed place, where many things are not in their place, when you walk, there are several things on the way, on the floor, in the kitchen: a total mess in your house. It might not look like it, but this completely affects your conscience and somehow stops you from working on your daily activities. Yes! Once you are in a place like that, your mind can tend to succumb to a general state of weird discouragement. That's because a disarrayed house makes you feel tired and leads you to procrastination.

Why is that if you got home with all the intention to finish? The answer is simple: You were having the intentions, and you were active, your mind and body were probably tired, but willpower and determination were stringer; nevertheless, once you get home and see all these things everywhere, and perceive the total mess, your mind saturates and reminds itself of how tired you are, then you come to be drowsy. It's a normal transition. Even if it's not time to go to bed, your mind and body were previously working. They must get tired and needed just one stimulus to get tired again and request rest. In this case, resting is a good option; notwithstanding, you lost the opportunity of when your mind and body were completely encouraged to keep working.

Habit #57

Read

Body is not everything and health does not imply only work out the body. You also have to work out your mind and improve your knowledge and intelligence. There's nothing better to do this than reading a book. It is considered one of the best habits a person may have and will definitely guide you to get your goals.

Reading opens the mind to new worlds and offers new life perspectives. It is always recommended to often read a book. You will learn from it and you will find different ways to perform your daily activities, besides, you can find encouragement in this, improve your reading and writing skills, your orthography and you'll feel more confident in any aspect of your life, due to the acquired knowledge.

Chapter 16

The Reasons You Have Trouble Creating Good Habits

So, you are in the zone. You are ready to make some changes to your life and throw out those bad habits. Everyone has a bad habit, although no one is willing to admit that they are not able to get rid of it. Whether your habit is watching too much TV, eating too much, drinking, being unorganized, or something else, you are now ready to get rid of that habit and switch to something that is better for your body and mind.

But sometimes the motivation is just not enough to get you going. You may have all the best intentions, but after just a few days, things start to get hard. You may consider yourself a strong person, capable of handling anything, but those urges and cravings start coming back and it is impossible to not run back to your old habit. It is usually within the first few days that people fail with all of the hard work that they are trying to accomplish.

Have you ever heard how it takes just 30 days to create a

new habit or to let go of an old one? You may have heard of this from those who are taking up a new exercise or doing a new habit that is good for them in some way. This is usually all it takes as long as you are able to stay the course and not let the bad habits creep back in. But this is also going to be one of the longest 30 days of your whole life.

Why is it so hard to get rid of some of those bad habits? Shouldn't your motivation and willpower be enough to get it all in order? Yes, these are often enough, but you also need to be able to convince the mind that the old habit is not a good thing and that you no longer want to participate in it. And your mind is a lot tougher than you think when it comes to giving up on habits.

The thing is, your mind wants to keep ahold of these habits. It doesn't recognize a habit as good or bad; instead, it recognizes that the habit you are doing is making life easier in some way. When you do things over and over again, the brain assumes this is a habit that is going to make you more efficient, regardless of whether the habit is good or not. It is going to latch on to that habit after a short amount of time, and you may find that it is extremely difficult to get things back on track.

When you decide it is time to get rid of the bad habits and go with the good ones, you are going to meet with some resistance. You have probably been partaking in those bad habits for years now and your brain is very comfortable with them. Now, you are trying to convince your brain that all of those habits from the past are no longer things that you want to do. The brain is going to resist and try to convince you to go back to the normal. Your brain does not like change and won't want you to give up something that it likes.

But you have to find the willpower to stick with it all. Yes, this is going to take some time and effort. You are now going to have to think about things before doing them. Before, with the bad habits, you were able to just go through life without a lot of thinking about your actions. But if you want to make a change, you need to think about the actions that you want to take and the ones that you want to avoid. You are probably going to spend the first week of this project thinking how easy it would be to just go backwards, but if you can get through a little bit longer, you will have a better chance at breaking the cycle of the bad habit and go on the path on being the person you want be with the habits you visualize yourself with. Remember "Motivation gets you started, habits get you going"

If you find that this is difficult to do, consider implementing a new habit at the same time. This allows the mind to focus and latch on to a new habit that will keep it safe and efficient so that it becomes easier to let things go. This makes it much easier to let go of the bad habit rather than just hoping the mind will forget about it.

Chapter 17

Surround Yourself with Positive People

Some of the friendships that you have made during the course of your life will have been good for you. There will have been others that are detrimental. If you find that you flinch each time the phone goes because you believe it will be a friend who wants something from you, then it's time to sort out your friendship habits.

Habit #58

Stop being a doormat

There is nothing as demotivating as being used as someone's doormat. This happens when you allow yourself to be used over and over again by the same people and find that these people give very little back to you in the way of friendship. It's time to learn to say "No." Although you will find this very hard at first, you do need to do it. What it will do is make you more respected and that's something you can't buy. Self-respect is vital to happiness and to health. You don't even need to explain why you cannot do as your friend is asking you, although if you lack confidence, chances are that you will want to have something ready to say, to explain your negative answer. Try telling your friend that you have "other arrangements" or that you are busy.

Habit #59

Start making positive friends

Write down a list of the things you fancy doing in your spare time. Then look to see if there are places near you where you can do these things. For instance, have you ever wanted to learn to dance? What about learning to improve your photography? Whatever it is that you like doing, try to find out if you can do this locally because you will meet people with a similar outlook if you go to places where these things happen. The local yoga club is a great place to meet positive people. What about joining the gym? Don't over extend yourself but give yourself things to do that you enjoy and where you mix with people who are positive and who are asking nothing from you.

Habit #60

Sorting out your friendships

Write the names of your friends onto a piece of paper and next to each of their names, add their characteristics.

For example:

- Jane – Friendly and good fun. Don't see her enough.

- Mary – Always miserable and asking for favors

- Ken – A bit of a plodder but honest and kind

- Mom – a little bit critical but nothing I can't handle

- Dad – Supportive and friendly, loves spending time with his grandkids

You can see that this is forming a pattern. You need to make a habit of being with people who make you happy and content more than you are with people who make you miserable. In the above case scenario, one could imagine that Mary isn't that good a friend. Depending upon past history, if you have a friendship that does all of the taking, then cut it out of your life – do it gradually if that helps, but do it. Don't get into the habit of being used. Ken is honest and kind and you probably have lots of friends like this, who may not be dynamic but who you can depend upon none-the-less. These are friends worth keeping.

Now look at your list and mark the friendships you need to cut down to minimum contact. I wouldn't mind betting that you have the bad habit of not staying in touch with some friends who actually mean a lot to you. Mark these as important and telephone each of them on a weekly basis, but use the opportunity as a positive experience. When you phone people who you have neglected for a long time, don't make the call about you. Make it about them. You owe them that. This makes them feel good about the fact that you got in touch and you never know, you may just be opening up possibilities for future contact by being the friend you should have been all along.

Habit #61

Volunteerism

Add something else to your list of friends. Perhaps you know people in your area who lives alone or who have plenty to be negative about. Each day, try to volunteer a little of your time to being nice to one of these people. For example, if you have an elderly neighbor who lives alone, why not bake them a cake. Get into the habit of being nice to people because if you do it without any other motive than their pleasure, you get so much self-worth from doing so. If you expect people to thank you or to reward you in some way, that's not true volunteering. Volunteering happens when you ask nothing in return. That's important. The habit of volunteerism helps you to adjust your own sense of self-worth and makes you feel great about life. It doesn't do that if you give with "strings" attached.

Chapter 18

Tips to Getting the Habit to Stick

Having some trouble getting started on your journey to making good habits. Don't sweat it! These things take time and they are going to be difficult. This is how our body works. To be efficient, you need to do the same things every day and when you try to change up the way that you act, your body and brain are going to resist. That doesn't mean you are going to fail. It simply means that you need a bit more motivation, practice, and time to make it all work for you.

If you are struggling, follow some of these easy tips to get you started:

Do it for 30 days

When you want to get started on a new habit or to drop an old one; just commit to 30 days. This is just a few weeks. While it might be some of the hardest weeks you have every dealt with, you will be able to get through all of this and see some results. If you can make it through the few weeks, you will see such an improvement in your life. Plus, your brain will start to see this new activity as a habit and you will just get up and do it without thinking.

Stick with it each day

You must stay consistent if you would like to get this habit to stick. For example, if you plan to start an exercise program, you need to try and make it to the gym each day for the first month. This might seem like a lot of overkill, but in the beginning, you are teaching your body that the gym is important and that you need to go. You can loosen this up a bit later on once you have made it a habit. But only working out three days a week may take longer to become a habit.

Start with something simple

Never try to change your life overnight. This is just not going to work. It is going to leave you frustrated and failing easier than before. Start out with something simple or set up milestones to help meet your goal.

Set a reminder

You will find that after two weeks, it becomes easier to forget about your goals. Don't let this happen otherwise you will begin to slip back into some of your old habits. Find a way to place reminders about the habit all around you so that you don't miss out on any days. Missing out on the activity is going to defeat all your hard work to start with.

Find a buddy

If you can find someone who will do the activity with you, this is going to make things so much easier. You will have someone who pushes you and is a motivating factor along for the whole ride. You have to hold yourself accountable when another person is present, making it harder to just give up or go back to the bad habits that you had before.

Find a trigger

This is basically some ritual that you are going to use right before you perform the new habit. An example of this is when you are trying to quit smoking. Whenever you feel like you want to have a cigarette, you could start snapping your fingers instead. If you plan on getting up earlier in the morning, you might want to implement the same rituals into the morning to make this process easier as your body gets used to the new routine.

It's ok to be imperfect

It is fine to fail once or twice along the way. Giving up an old habit is tough. You don't want to beat yourself up too much over all this or you may feel like it is all hopeless. Realize that mistakes are going to happen and that these mistakes are not the end of the world. This takes off some of the pressure and makes it easier to dust yourself off and get back to work after you fall.

Get rid of the temptation

Try to change your environment as much as possible so that you aren't being tempted by the things that will get you back onto your old habits. You can get rid of those cigarettes if you want to stop smoking, cancel the cable if you want to be more active and stop watching TV, or get rid of the bad foods if you are on a diet. When you get rid of the temptations, it is much easier for you to stick with your plans and see some results. While you are at this, make sure to find something that will stand in as comfort when you are done. If TV or cigarettes were a way to calm you down, it is going to be almost impossible to calm down without them during these 30 days. Consider meditation, reading, or some type of exercise to keep yourself relaxed and away from the bad habit.

Do it as an experiment

Worried about failing when you try out this process? Take a different approach. Do everything that you would need to in order to get rid of your bad habit or add in a new one for the 30 days. Don't have judgment against yourself during this time. Just see this as an experiment to determine how well you can do the process. It is not possible to fail when you are doing an experiment, so you won't feel so terrible when things don't go your way 100 percent. And at the end, it is likely that you have developed the new habit that you want.

Do it because you want to

When forming a new habit, do not concentrate on the reasons that you should do the habit or all of the other habits that you should be working on. This is not going to make you feel good about yourself. These are just going to be full of empty resolutions that will never become fulfilled because you don't care all that much but will still make you feel bad because of the guilt. Rather than letting this get to you, find a habit that you would like to implement into your life, one that you are passionate about, and work towards that.

Getting a good habit to stick can be a challenge. You are going to need to work hard to see results and it will not happen overnight. But when you try out some of these tips and stick with your resolutions, you will soon see that good habit become a part of your regular routine without having to think about it.

Conclusion

Selective focus is good, smart focus is better. You need to remember at all times that if you're not giving the job at hand your all, it will never rise to your expectation. Even if the job is small, give it all your attention and give it all your time. The functional word here is 'prioritize.' This is why I talk about smart focus. Analyze what needs your immediate attention and then dedicate all your attention to it.

Environment plays a very important work in helping you focus. If you feel like you can't work at home, pull an all-nighter at your office. If it's the festive season, make sure you make arrangements in advance to find yourself a quiet isolated spot that leaves you alone with your work.

Once you've prioritized and settled to work don't stray. It's a good habit to take small breaks, in fact it's healthy. But the job has to be done no matter what, and getting distracted mid-way can lead to procrastination. Remember the old adage, better now than never? Implement it.

Staying focused also allows you to take up one small goal at a time. This allows you to simply work towards one minor attainable achievement rather than worry about the bigger picture. Let this achievement breed confidence that carries you through other short-term goals and finally to the ultimate goal.

Not being aware of our habits doesn't mean that they don't exist. Every person has a set of habits, positive or negative, and the only reason we are not thinking about them is because they have become an automated part of who we are. We are so used to having a particular behavior that we don't even notice when we are performing some habits.

When it comes to negative habits this can be a real disadvantage. It takes a lot of training and self-awareness to realize when you start doing something negative out of habit and in an automatic manner.

Be aware of negative habits but do not focus on them. You see, reverse psychology works very well for our brain, the exact things we try not to do usually end up being the things we will do, almost certainly.

If you have a habit you want to stop, it is best to focus on developing a habit that will turn you into the person you want to be. So instead of wasting energy to erase a habit, it is more efficient to create a replacement habit that will be better and safer for you.

Is it possible not to have habits at all? Well, not really, because this is how we are built. Our brain looks for a way to save energy and be more efficient when working, so the things we do most often, as a part of our daily routine, are the ones that usually end up as becoming habits.

The contents of this book may not be reproduced, duplicated or transmitted without direct written permission from the author.

Under no circumstances will any legal responsibility or blame be held against the publisher for any reparation, damages, or monetary loss due to the information herein, either directly or indirectly.

Legal Notice:

This book is copyright protected. This is only for personal use. You cannot amend, distribute, sell, use, quote or paraphrase any part or the content within this book without the consent of the author.

Disclaimer Notice:

Please note the information contained within this document is for educational and entertainment purposes only. Every attempt has been made to provide accurate, up to date and reliable complete information. No warranties of any kind are expressed or implied. Readers acknowledge that the author is not engaging in the rendering of legal, financial, medical or professional advice. The content of this book has been derived from various sources. Please consult a licensed professional before attempting any techniques outlined in this book.

By reading this document, the reader agrees that under no circumstances are is the author responsible for any losses, direct or indirect, which are incurred as a result of the use of information contained within this document, including, but not limited to, —errors, omissions, or inaccuracies.

© Copyright 2017 Dibbly Publishing.
All rights reserved.

Table of Contents

INTRODUCTION 1

CHAPTER 1 HOW DO I KNOW IF I AM PROCRASTINATING? 5

CHAPTER 2 WHY DO I PROCRASTINATE? 15
- LACK OF MOTIVATION 15
- FEAR OF FAILURE 18
- SKILLS DEFICIT 20
- FEELING OVERWHELMED 22

CHAPTER 3 THE CYCLE OF PROCRASTINATION 25

CHAPTER 4 START SMALL. GROW BIG. 37

CHAPTER 5 PARKINSON'S LAW 47
- HARD WORK VS SMART WORK 52

CHAPTER 6 THE LAW OF THREE 59
- PARETO PRINCIPLE 59
- PARKINSON'S LAW AND THE POMODORO TECHNIQUE 65
- NEWTON'S FIRST LAW OF MOTION 74

CHAPTER 7 REWARDS 77

CHAPTER 8 WORKING WITH YOURSELF 85

CONCLUSION 99

Introduction

Procrastination is something everyone has encountered in their lives. Whether you have left a term project for the last minute, or you're still waiting to find the resolve to start your new fitness program, you know what it means to struggle to get certain tasks done.

For some people, procrastination is more than leaving certain tasks to the last minute. Procrastination has become a way of life for them. While people tend to joke about their tendency to procrastinate, I believe that it is time we treat procrastination as the potentially harmful habit it is.

When you live a life of constantly failing to meet expectations and fulfill goals, you hinder yourself from becoming successful. Success is directly relate to the way you handle your day-to-day tasks. If your day-to-day tasks are not completed in the time you are meant to have completed them, this can causes serious problems for you in the future.

The reason why I wrote this book is to help people who have struggled with procrastination for a greater part of their lives.

Don't think of your book as a guide to showing you all the areas in which you are going wrong. That is the total opposite of what this book is set out to do. Picture this as a conversation between you and someone who cares about your progress. Overcoming a habit can be a very challenging thing - that is understandable. Sometimes, the reason why people feel as if they are unable to grow in their personal development is because they feel that they are alone. People would rather live with their regressive habits instead of setting out to better themselves because they feel that they don't have the support from people around you. Well, if that is your case, I would like you to know that I do support you. That is why I chose to write this book.

I understand the difficulties one faces in trying to overcome a habit other people often see as a burden and not a struggle. Procrastination affects every area of a person's life – including in their relationships. Maybe the people in your life have lost their faith in you as a result of your compulsive need to procrastinate. You are probably at a point where you are tired of making excuses for your behavior.

The first step to overcoming a problem is acknowledging that you need to overcome it. People often try to minimalize their struggles in order to appear as if they are in control. There is no need to pretend here. This book is meant to provide you with a safe space to understand why you do the things that you do.

Many people don't understand why they procrastinate. They simply think that it is because they don't know how to manage time. Some people believe that their procrastination is a result of their laziness.

While this may be true for some cases, it isn't the case for everyone.

In this book, you will find ways to identify the root causes of your procrastination. The book includes descriptive information that will assist you with finding ways to deal with these root causes in order to stop procrastinating. You will find this statement in many parts of the book: there is more to procrastination than not knowing how to keep to time.

This book will also provide you with practical ways to deal with your habit. There are a variety of methods that you can try out. Some of them are simple and straightforward. Most of them have to do with your mind and the way it functions.

The main focus of everything that you will find in this book is for you to become a more organized and focused person in order to live a more fulfilling and successful life.

Chapter 1
How Do I Know if I am Procrastinating?

Before a problem can be solved, one has to acknowledge that there actually is a problem that needs to be dealt with. In order for you to overcome chronic procrastination, you need to acknowledge that you actually are a chronic (or serial) procrastinator. Listed below, are the main characteristics of a serial procrastinator. Fictional scenarios have been added to every point in order to give you a clearer picture of what it means to be a serial procrastinator.

- **You are always leaving tasks to the last minute.**

    Luna checks the time. It's two o'clock in the morning and she has three more assignments to finish before the sun rises. She takes a sip from her fourth cup of coffee and proceeds with her work. She looks at the numerous tabs opened on her browser and sighs. "Where did all the time go?" she wonders as she reflects on the amount of work she needs to finish within the next few hours.

Serial procrastinators tend to leave major tasks to the last minute, which is usually a few days before the tasks are due. They often deceive themselves into thinking that they are leaving the tasks to later, so that they can give these tasks their undivided attention. Serial procrastinators tend to look at their workload and determine that they can finish it "later". This is how they find themselves hurriedly handling tasks in the wee hours of the morning as a result of constantly putting off tasks that could have been done earlier.

- **You are always in a rush.**

    The alarm clock goes off. Mike's hand shoots out from under the sheets and pushes the alarm clock off of the bedside table. His phone starts to ring minutes later. He sits up and picks up his phone. One of his work colleagues is calling to remind him of the early morning meeting that is due to start in the next ninety minutes. Mike ends the call, jumps out of bed, and rushes to the shower. He attempts to shower and brush his teeth at the same time, whilst trying to remember the venue for the meeting. He steps out of the shower and heads straight to his closet. His phone is ringing again. Halfway through pulling on his pants, Mike hops to his phone and answers the call. It's his work colleague again, reminding him of the meeting's venue and the files that need to be brought to the meeting. Mike ends the call, dresses up in five minutes and rushes to the kitchen. He throws open his briefcase and pulls out the relevant files whilst grabbing an apple at the same time. He makes a mental note to buy groceries in the evening – this is the third day in a row that he's had to remind himself of this. It takes Mike another five minutes to pack his things and leave the apartment. He jogs to his car, throws in his belongings and speeds off to his meeting. During the drive to the venue, he tries to remember the number of tasks he needs to complete before the day is over. A number of memos are flashing on his phone; reminding him of week-long work that needs to be completed within the next couple of days.

Due to their inability to manage their time well, serial procrastinators are often in a rush. Poor time management forces them to try and finish due tasks in a short space of time, whilst trying to balance the rest of their tasks. If you find that you are always in a rush because you are unable to manage your time well, this means that there is a high chance that you are a serial procrastinator.

- **You focus on numerous unimportant tasks before attempting to work on the main task.**

Sam has been assigned a law assignment that needs to be submitted at 8am the next day. Determined to finish it on time, he sets his laptop before him and opens the assignment. After perusing it for a couple of minutes, he minimizes the window and decides to clean up his emails. "My inbox is a mess," he mumbles to himself as he goes through the unread messages and deletes the irrelevant ones. His inbox is cleared in thirty minutes. Feeling good about himself, he decides to tidy up his Facebook Messenger inbox too. One hour later, he returns to his assignment and takes a look at it. He types a couple of sentences before he takes a minute to think of something else to do. He looks around his room and realizes how stuffy it is. He opens the window and looks at the clutter on the floor. "I need to clean this up," he says, as he bends down and starts to clear the floor. Another hour passes by and he feels good about the new state of his room. He sits at his desk again and works on his assignment for five minutes. His phone flashes and he reads the incoming message; after he has read the message he takes a look at his applications and realizes that most of them need to be updated. An hour passes by before all his applications have been updated. Sam takes a look at the time and is surprised to find that it's already nighttime. "Where did all the time go?" he wonders. Realizing that he is running out of time, he begins to work on his assignment again.

Serial procrastinators are known to fill their time with menial tasks instead of tackling the major tasks that need their attention. Convinced that they "can do it later", they spend their time working on meaningless activities that could be done much later. If you find yourself focusing on irrelevant tasks, instead of working on more important projects and assignments, you might be a serial procrastinator.

- **You are always burnt out**

  Amy falls into her chair and lets out a huge sigh. She picks up her compact mirror and takes a look at her face. She groans as she looks at the dark bags under her eyes and her flaking skin. She was unable to cover her face with concealer because she overslept. Amy throws the mirror to the side and looks at the pile of folders on her desk. She has several reports that are due in the next couple of days and she knows that she is about to receive more work from her boss. She bites her half-broken nail while she waits for her computer to turn on. A flurry of emails fill her screen and she closes her tired eyes. Her day is filled with meetings and she's not sure how she's going to cope with the heavy workload. Amy pinches the bridge of her nose, closes her eyes, and wonders why she didn't complete her work over the weekend.

  Burnout is common among serial procrastinators. The late nights and constant pressure that they find themselves under ends up having an effect on their health. Lack of sleep and constant stress leads to fatigue, poor concentration, and an inability to function effectively. Serial procrastinators often have bags under their eyes, due to the late nights, and are often plagued by guilt when they realize that their heavy workload is a result of their inability to do their work on time. If you find yourself feeling burnt out on a regular basis, and it traces back to your inability to complete yours tasks in good time, then this is a sign that you might be a serial procrastinator.

- **You are convinced that you work better under pressure**

  Andrew's laptop pinged. He took a look at the email – another assignment due. He opened the file and perused it for a couple of minutes. It was going to take him three days to complete the assignment. He did a mental check of the other projects he needed to complete; they were all due the following week. Andrew looked at the assignment in front of him and minimized the window. He would do it the following week. Andrew always spoke of how he was unable to complete his work in advance. "I work well when I am under pressure," was his standard statement. Andrew nodded his head, turned off his laptop, and headed to the canteen for an early break.

  A number of people who claim to swear by the "no sleep, all work" rhetoric – which claims that only successful people are capable of working until the sunrises – are actually people who have left their projects and tasks to the last minute. Serial procrastinators often suffer from insufficient sleep due to the long hours they spent, trying to catch up on all of the work that they had left for later. If you find yourself feeling tired throughout the day, as a result of too many late nights, you need to take time to find the root cause for this.

A heavy workload is often a result of poor time management; and poor time management is a by-product of continuous procrastination. As I mentioned in the previous chapter, it is very hard to clear a backlog of tasks while you are receiving new assignments that require you attention. Procrastination will have you thinking that you will be able finish all of your assignments, projects, or tasks in a short period of time. If you find that a heavy workload is the reason why you are always working hurriedly, on a regular basis, you might be a serial procrastinator.

- **You are full of excuses**

    "Everyone, I am so sorry but this is the last time my work will be late," Zach pleaded. "Something came up and I wasn't able to finish the last couple of pages on time. You know how crazy this place gets!"

Zach's colleagues watched him wearily. This was the fourth time in two months that he hadn't submitted work on time. They were used to his excuses and none of them had the energy to call him out on his shoddy behavior. Alicia, the head of the team, sighed and looked at Zach for a couple of minutes. She waved her hand flippantly and asked him to sit down. Zach sat down, hurriedly, and returned to his laptop. He had several emails from clients, asking him for a progress report on the work he was doing for them. Zach typed furiously, profusely apologizing to every single client and assuring them that their work will be in on time. He hadn't started any of the tasks, yet. He looked at his watch and noted the time. He had a meeting with his supervisor in fifteen minutes. He gathered his papers together and left the office. Everyone in the workplace knew that Zach was incapable of sticking to deadlines. Instead of owning up to his actions, Zach was always giving excuses for his inability to complete work on time. What baffled his colleagues even more, was his eagerness to accept more work – despite the other work he had not completed.

Serial procrastinators are known to make excuses for their inability to fulfill tasks on time. They will give you excuses as to why they haven't joined the gym yet; why their work is always late; and why they never arrive on time. If you know that you give excuses for unfulfilled tasks on a regular basis, this may be a sign that you are a serial procrastinator.

Procrastinating is not exclusive to corporate work or schoolwork. How many times have you postponed your new fitness program? How long does it take you to get up and do something you've been meaning to do for hours?

If you can relate to more than two or three of the above mentioned characteristics, and you know that there are many things that you haven't done in your life as a result of procrastination, then you need to acknowledge that you have a problem that needs to be dealt with.

Chapter 2
Why Do I Procrastinate?

In the previous chapter, you went through the characteristics that are typically found in serial procrastinators. This chapter is dedicated to unravelling the reasons behind the actions. Most people who struggle with procrastination often state that they don't know why they procrastinate so much. In most cases, this statement is true. It takes active reflection for one to determine the motives behind their actions. If you are one of those procrastinators who doesn't know why they do what they do, this chapter will help shed a little light on the reasons behind your actions. If you are aware of the reasons you procrastinate, read along anyway. You'll definitely learn something that might help you in this journey of growth and overcoming.

Lack of Motivation

Lack of motivation plays a major role in why people choose to procrastinate. Many people believe that they can only work when they are motivated or inspired. If that determined buzz is not there, neither is their productivity. Instead of trying to do the task, regardless of how they may be feeling, procrastinators spend their time focusing on less important tasks. They call this "waiting for inspiration". When asked about when the inspiration or motivation is expected to arrive, procrastinators will often shrug and say that they are not sure. This is common, but not exclusive to, people who work in the creative field.

For some people, motivation is a tangible feeling that they are aware of. They believe that, in order for them to produce good work they need to feel as motivated as possible. Some of the unimportant tasks procrastinators may partake in are listening to music or watching videos that they believe will "motivate" them into working. Procrastinators tend to deceive themselves, knowingly and/or unknowingly, by thinking that their attempts to "motivate" themselves are productive. These activities are often counterproductive because they end up taking up the time the procrastinator could have used to complete the tasks they needed to complete in the first place.

Lack of motivation can also be traced back to an attitude problem. Procrastination is not hereditary; it is a learned habit. "I don't feel like doing it" isn't just a statement. It is a reflection of one's attitude towards work. If a person bases their rate of productivity on whether they feel like it or not, instead of the importance of the task's completion, this shows that there is an imbalance in priorities. If you are a procrastinator whose motives are often feeling-based, you will find yourself unconsciously sabotaging your work ethic. The belief that one needs motivation in order to work effectively, is a damaging belief to hold.

This is the reason why people find themselves plateauing in their careers, schoolwork, or extracurricular activities. Personal growth requires going the extra mile. Going the extra mile means that you are willing to overlook your feelings and emotions in order to achieve your desired goal. If you substitute that extra effort for using that effort to partake in distractions, you will always end up on the wrong side of your goals. Procrastinators tend to view tasks as demotivating for a number of reasons, and because of this, they don't view them as important – no matter how important they are in actuality.

It is usually the "boring" and challenging tasks that will have a person feeling demotivated. Handling unpleasant situations, tedious tasks like paying taxes, or completing demanding assignments are the types of activities that people demotivated about. These tasks are often seen as less exciting and/or inspiring. But to believe that you need to feel charged or motivated in order to complete them, will end up having a reverse-effect on your ability to complete these tasks. The task ends up being dragged out for longer than it should have in the first place.

Fear of Failure

The fear of failure is another reason why people tend to procrastinate.

Failure is inevitable in every person's life. It's nearly impossible to getting something right the first time round. While some people are able to shake it off and try again, others are not. The negative experience ends up having a hold on the person, and they find themselves unable to try again. In situations where they are required to try again, for example, a second assignment, the person resorts to putting off the task for as long as they possibly can. The fear of failure compels them to avoid the task because they don't want to experience the hurt or disappointment again.

Sometimes people sabotage themselves on purpose, in order to have an explanation for why their work isn't as good as it should be. It is a warped way of trying to combat the fear of prospective failure. A person will leave the task to the last minute, work on it hurriedly, and then claim that the reason why the work isn't as good as it should be is because they did not give themselves enough time to focus on the task. Sometimes a person will soothe themselves by saying, "I would have done so much better if I had more time," not realizing that the reason why they didn't have enough time was because of their own actions.

Some people view their procrastination as a way of

protecting themselves from failure. If they are ruled by thoughts like "The last time I put in all that effort, I failed. I'm not going to do that again." This is why people tend to struggle with reviving their fitness regimes, business ideas, or even their assignments in college. Failure can leave a lasting impression on a person and it takes a lot for them to overcome it. The fear and disappointment the person experienced at that time, may contribute to the reason why they leave their work for the last minute.

The underlying factor, when it comes to the fear of failure, is perfectionism. People who identify as perfectionists also tend to be serial procrastinators. Thoughts of doing the task perfectly, or at the right time, often end up taking up a person's time. Perfectionists tend to be plagued by the fear of not doing the task properly and this leads to putting the task off. When it's the last minute, and they can no longer put off the task, they rush it and try to do as best as they can. If everything works out, they are satisfied. But if the project does not meet their desired expectations, they put the blame on the insufficient time they had.

Sometimes people will fill their schedules with various "busy" tasks in order to give themselves the illusion that the fact that they have to do the work at the last minute is out of their control. The fear of failing other people may also come into play when a person procrastinates. The thought of disappointing other people consumes their time and leaves them without the energy to focus on the task at hand.

Skills Deficit

If you lack the required skills to complete a certain task, there is a high chance that you are going to put off the task for as long as you possibly can.

For example, if you have to read a book for a Literature assignment, and you happen to be a slow reader, you might be phased by your inability to read fast. Feelings of inadequacy or discouragement may overwhelm you and you will end up avoiding the task for as long as possible. Skills deficit is one of the most common reasons for procrastination. When one is faced with a task that requires a skill one may be lacking, one will try to leave the task for as late as possible. A person will do this because they lack the motivation to try and handle such a challenging task.

The fear of failure will also come to play here because a person may feel that if they try to work on the task, they will fail. A person who hasn't run in years might put off going to the gym because they feel that they aren't fit enough to maintain a regular regime. It may sound insignificant to an outsider, but these thoughts are very serious to the person who is doubting themselves. Sometimes, the skills deficit might be in a person's head.

Due to things like previous failures and insecurities, a person may feel that they aren't skilled enough to complete a task, thus putting it off for as long as possible.

A person might end up spending most of their time giving themselves multiple reasons as to why they are incapable of doing the project successfully. They may use a set of excuses to justify their procrastination and most of these excuses will revolve around the fact that the task does not play to their strengths. For example, a person might hold off on setting up a budget because they aren't good with calculations. Instead of trying to find someone to help them, they choose to leave the task for later. The task ends up being done in a rush or, in some instances, it is never completed.

The reason why people tend to keep quiet about their lacking skills is because they don't want to be looked down upon. For example, a slow reader might not want to admit this out loud because they fear that they will be insulted by their peers. Instead of seeking help, procrastinators would prefer to keep their struggles to themselves and leave the work for a later time. If the work isn't of great importance, they will simply put off the task until they have forgotten about it. The main goal being that they won't have to confront the areas in which they are lacking.

Some people tend to see procrastination as the better option - as opposed to dealing with the challenging task hands-on. Procrastination, to them, means that they aren't giving up on the task; they are simply leaving it for a better time. This is another example of mental deception. It is also self-sabotaging because the only thing the person has achieved is creating a backlog of work. When the person is faced with another task that requires that same skill they feel they are lacking in, they will put off that task too. Eventually, the person might be faced with a number of challenging tasks that need to be completed in more time than they actually have.

Feeling Overwhelmed

Lastly, another reason why a person might procrastinate is because they feel overwhelmed by what is required of them – especially if any of the other aforementioned reasons for procrastination are at play. If a person feels that they lack the adequate skills to successful complete a task, they may feel overwhelmed at the thought of having to do the task in the first place. The fear of failure might be amplified in a situation like this. Instead of reaching out for assistance, the person will choose to put off the task instead. To them, they are simply leaving it for a time where they feel more confident but this rarely ever happens. In most cases, the task is completed hurriedly, at the last minute, or it is left incomplete.

In another instance, a person might end up feeling overwhelmed because of their heavy workload – which is usually a result of prior procrastination. Feelings of guilt and regret tend to come up in times like this and the person ends up avoiding the work altogether, instead of trying to tackle the work at hand. At some point, the work can appear to be too much for a person – no matter how much confidence they have in their ability to work well under pressure. Something always gives in. The late nights, the piles of work, and the anxiety caused by the pressure, will end up having an effect on a person. Work becomes overwhelming and they end up feeling like they cannot cope.

When a person feels overwhelmed, their ability to mentally process things effectively reduces. It's in situations like this where a person ends up following their emotions instead of practicality. The practical solution would be trying to find a way to navigate through the heavy workload. But when a person is feeling overwhelmed, if they are unable to think logically all they will want is to get rid of the problem as fast as possible. Enter procrastination. Putting off the work – *again* – seems like the best option in that instant because it will temporarily deal with the overwhelming feeling. This feeling will end up returning, eventually, because at some point the work has to be done.

As you can see from the reasons above, procrastination is more than just a physical thing. The mind has a lot to do with a person's struggle with procrastination. Attitudes, beliefs, and insecurities all stem from the mind. This shows that when one has to overcome procrastination, a large part of the battle will take place in their mind.

Chapter 3
The Cycle of Procrastination

Procrastination is not just about the single act of procrastinating. There is a cycle that takes place that the procrastinator might not be (consciously) aware of. In this chapter, the cycle of procrastination has been broken down for you to understand and identify with. The cycle occurs in the following eight stages:

1. **Approaching a Task**

    The cycle begins with approaching a task that needs to be completed. The task can come in various forms – a work assignment; a term project; joining the gym; paying bills etc. The task can be newly-given or one that was given at an earlier time; either way, the task needs to be completed. This stage also consists of assessing the task, considering the amount of focus the task requires, and taking note of the time frame in which the task needs to be completed. Once the task has been assessed, one begins to contemplate how they are going to handle the task.

In this stage, the desire to complete the task is present. The person wants to do the task and they are trying to find a way to start. The task may be examined a couple of times, light research may be done where necessary and a few notes may be taken. If it's an extracurricular or errand-related activity, a few phone calls may be made or the person may try to map out how they are going to carry out the task. No significant work is done during this stage. The person is simply gauging what is before them. They might evaluate the task against the other things that they need to do – some being a result of previous procrastination. In this stage, a person with incentive would make an active attempt to get started with the work. They would go beyond doing light research or evaluations; they would dive into the work. A procrastinator, however, will start to experience reservations based on assumptions and rules they have held for a long time.

2. Assumptions and Rules

The assumptions and rules that come into play here are the motives and reasons that were discussed in the previous chapter. Once the person starts to assess or attempt to work on the task at hand, these thoughts and beliefs start to manifest. Whilst the person is thinking of how to approach the task, their fear of failure may be triggered and their thoughts change. Instead of thinking of how they can handle the task, their minds are consumed by the prospects of working on the task and failing. Memories from previous experiences join these thoughts and the motivation the person had before starts to dwindle.

Other feelings like the feeling of uncertainty or an awareness of one's skills deficit will be roused as well. The person's incentive to get started on the task dwindles as they pay attention to the assumptions and rules that determine the way they work. Not long after these thoughts have entered their mind, the person makes a decision that they can do the work later. Later rarely has a specific time attached to it. A sense of faux confidence could come into play as well. Thoughts like "I work better under pressure" and other thoughts that underestimate the focus the task requires quell the sense of urgency the person had at the beginning. Their assumptions are further supported by thoughts of previous tasks they finished at the last minute that turned out to be successful. "If I could do it back then,

I can definitely do it again."

3. Discomfort, Repel, Avoid

The feelings roused by the person's assumptions and mental rules will make them feel uncomfortable. The thought of doing the project daunts them. They do not have any motivation to counter these feelings and they start to search for a way out. For example, if a person is faced with the task of spring cleaning their sitting room, their initial sense of urgency will be replaced by their feeling overwhelmed by the task before them. The thought of spending so much time clearing out the sitting room makes them want to drop everything and leave the house. This is because of the thoughts that entered their minds when they were assessing the task at hand.

A strong desire to repel the task will be catalyzed by the discomfort the person was feeling earlier. They will start looking for reasons to put off the task. Their thoughts shift from focusing on the discomfort of the task, to alternative activities that will soothe their discomfort. The person might think of other "important" activities they can busy themselves with instead of clearing the sitting room. A sudden inspiration to visit the bookstore might come upon them. The person will go on to come up with reasons as to why this task is far more beneficial than the original task they were meant to be focusing on.

Once they have come up with the assurance they need, the person will abandon the initial task and leave it for a later time. Instead of figuring out when that later time is, the person proceeds to focus on the less important tasks.

4. Excuses

During the period of procrastination, a serial procrastinator will feel guilty about their actions. Thoughts of the times the procrastinated before will fill their mind and they will pause to reflect on their actions. They will feel guilty for choosing to put off another task instead of dealing with it from the get-go. They may take a moment to question their actions and consider reversing their decision. For example, if a person chose to go to the mall instead of spring cleaning their sitting room, they might feel guilty for doing so. They will take a moment to consider leaving the bookstore and returning home to clean the sitting room, like they'd initially planned.

In order to stave off the guilt, the person will come up with excuses that will justify their procrastination. They will convince themselves that the task isn't that demanding and they will be able to finish it quickly when they finally decide to handle it. If the fear of failure is driving their procrastination, they will soothe their guilt by reminding themselves of the times they tried to work hard and it did not work out. If the person feels that they don't have the adequate skills to complete the task successfully, they will use this as an excuse to justify putting off the task. They will convince themselves that they need to take care of other easier tasks before they try and deal with the more challenging one. The end result of this stage is that the person will overcome their guilt and continue with their procrastination.

5. Distractions

To keep the guilt at bay, the procrastinator will turn to different kinds of distractions in order to keep themselves "busy". For example, once the person has completed what they've had to do at the bookstore, instead of returning home to spring clean the sitting room, they will go to a different store and focus on hanging around there. If they don't have anything constructive to do in that store, they will resort to wandering around aimlessly and examining the things that are on sale. In their minds, they are convinced that what they are doing is just as important as what they were meant to be doing at home.

The purpose of these distractions is to keep the person active and convinced that they are being productive. Procrastinators are often aware that what they are doing is wrong. In order to curb the awareness of their actions, they fill their time with trivial activities. For most adults, their distractions are often the applications on their phones and laptops, and social media. Procrastinators tend to become so absorbed by their distractions, they actually forget about what they are meant to be doing. If care isn't taken, a significant amount of time passes by before the procrastinator realizes that they have something that needs to be done within a certain period of time. At this point, the procrastinator can choose to abandon their distractions and go back to the initial task, or they can shrug off their feelings and continue with their distractions.

6. Consequences

Eventually, there comes a point where the person can no longer avoid the task. They run out of time and they realize that they have to handle the task. By the time a procrastinator realizes this, they don't have much time on their hands. This is where the late nights and rushed hours come into the equation. Most procrastinators end up sacrificing sleep in order to complete the task they should have done long before. In the continuous example we have used in this chapter, a person might only resort to spring cleaning the sitting room hours before they are expecting visitors, or after they have contracted hay fever. By then, their efforts are harried and they are working under immense pressure. Panic interferes with their thought pattern and completing the task becomes more challenging than it was at the beginning.

There can be positive consequences of a procrastinator's actions, though. For those who have become accustomed to working under such strenuous conditions, they will get the job done and will experience great relief after the completion of the task. They may have a sense of accomplishment and they might be encouraged to complete a few more tasks. Any guilt they may have felt whilst rushing to complete the task will vanish and they will continue with their other tasks.

The negative consequences, however, tend to outweigh the positives when it comes to procrastination. Even if the person manages to successfully complete the task at the last minute, the effects from the late nights and the stress will take a toll on them. If task is not work-related, the person will have to deal with the consequences that come with the unfulfilled tasks. Despite their earlier confidence in their actions, the reality of their failure, which was due to their own actions, will sink in.

7. Guilt and a resolve to change

After reflecting on the negative consequences of their actions, procrastinators will end up feeling guilty for what they've done. They will spend time reflecting on the repercussions of their actions. Even if they managed to successfully complete the task, procrastinators will still have to deal with the negative effects the last minute rush had on their mental and physical state. Fatigue and disappointment are often the main things a procrastinator will feel after they've finally managed to deal with the task at hand. If they procrastinated to the point that the task remained incomplete, procrastinators are faced with the reality of their actions. A procrastinator's actions inevitably end up affecting people around them as well. A client ends up being disappointed, a team is let down, or someone is left with shoddy work because of the procrastinator's actions. If the situation isn't resolved, the trust people had in these procrastinators dwindle. Being faced with people's disappointment further intensifies the guilt that the procrastinators' were feeling initially. No one likes disappointing the people who have trust in them.

In these situations, procrastinators resolve to change their actions and refrain from procrastinating again. The negative consequences of their actions are the driving force behind their journey towards redemption. They will spend the next couple of days planning on ways to eliminate the distractions from their lives so that they can fully focus on the rest of the tasks that need to be completed. Procrastinators can go as far as trying to schedule their lives effectively, in order to complete all of their tasks in good time.

8. **The cycle continues.**

The problem with the many procrastinators' attempts at seeking redemption is that they don't tackle the problem from the roots. To them, they believe that they have a time management problem and they try to curb that. After reading the previous chapter, you should realize that procrastination is more than poor time management. If anything, poor time management is simply a by-product of procrastination; it rarely is the root cause. Since the root of the matter is not being confronted, a procrastinator's attempts to fix their problem end up becoming ineffective. As time goes by, the procrastinator begins to let go of their attempts to improve, and they slowly slip back to their old habits. After a while, the procrastinator is back to doing what they do best – procrastinating – and the cycle continues.

Chapter 4
Start Small. Grow Big.

In the last point of the previous chapter, I mentioned the struggle that many procrastinators encounter when they attempt to make a change to their ways. When they try to curb their tendency to procrastinate, they only approach the surface of the issue. On the surface, procrastination may seem like it is a result of poor time management and substandard organizational skills. This is why you will find procrastinators resorting to purchasing alarm clocks, downloading scheduling apps, and setting numerous reminders for themselves. They believe that if they take care of the surface-level problems (poor time management, delayed action, etc.) then they will be able to take care of the whole problem (procrastination). But this rarely happens. Their high-energy will last for a certain period of time before they fall back to their old ways. This is by no means an attack on anyone who is trying to improve their lives, no.

But anyone who is struggling with a habit that is detrimental to their wellbeing -and the way they function - needs to realize that they are going to need to change the way they've been trying to do things in the first place. Procrastination is rarely ever just a surface problem, especially if it is a habit that a person has had for many years. At some point, procrastination is capable of affecting a person's life on a larger scale than imagined. It is possible for one to view procrastination as part of their personality. At this point, a person might not be able to find the resolve to deal with the problem. It's very hard for a person to attempt to overcome the things that they feel are a part of their identity. This is how deeply-rooted a problem procrastination can be. It is not just about poor time management and making excuses. When you tell a person to get their act together and learn how to manage their time, you are not helping them. One cannot simply turn off the "procrastinate" switch and flip on another switch that allows them to work effectively. Unfortunately, it is not that simple.

"The journey of a thousand miles begins with one step."

– Lao Tzu

In order to overcome a big problem, you have to tackle it bit by bit. Attempting to deal with a problem by taking it on headfirst will always result in failure. When it comes to procrastination, the same thing applies here. In order for you to overcome your problematic habit of being unable to finish anything on time, you have to tackle the problem one bit at a time. The fact that your problem has reached this stage means that a number of small decisions were made and a number of actions took place until they all accumulated into the habit that you have today. It's going to take a lot more than scheduling apps and daily reminders for you to overcome your procrastination. This shouldn't make you feel as if there is no hope, though. We are just going through the reality of your situation. By doing this, we are helping you realize that it is going to take a number of small-scale steps for you to effect a long-lasting change in your life.

Turning your habit around is going to take time. It took a considerable amount of time for your habit to get where it is today. Ideally, it is going to take time for you to reverse that habit and create a healthier and more beneficial lifestyle for yourself. The sooner you realize this, the better. Sometimes it can become a little demotivating when you look at your progress after a certain amount of time and you find that it is not where you would want it to be. Change takes time. If you want the change to last for the rest of your life, then you need to realize that it's going to take a considerable amount of time for that change to effectively take place in your life. There is no quick-fix for procrastination. There is no such thing as a quick-fix solution for anything, really. Quick-fix solutions are a scam. After a while, the "fix" unravels and you'll find that the problem has become far worse than what it was in the beginning. This book is not a quick-fix solution for procrastinators. This book will guide you through the right way to overcome a habit of procrastination.

This is why you have to see that the best way to handle the problem is to start with a "small" approach.

Some of the "start small tactics" that a person can use will be similar to the tactics a person uses to deal with the "surface problems" of procrastination. The reason why these tactics are seen as small is because they are meant to be carried out individually. Change is a gradual thing. If you try to change your lifestyle full speed ahead, you will end up failing. Take it one step at a time – bit by bit.

1. Write down all the tasks that you need to do for the day.

This is an easy task to start off with and it is also a way to start dealing with the overwhelming feeling you get that leads you to putting off tasks. It will also help you with your organizational skills. Purchase a notebook and use it to take note of the tasks that need to be completed throughout the day. *Do not use your phone.* Mobile phones are filled with a variety of applications that will end up serving as distractions instead of aides. There is also something about writing down your to-do list that helps you calm down. When you leave everything in your mind, it becomes much easier for you to become overwhelmed. When you see everything on paper, it's easier for you to see what needs to be done first and what can wait. When you manage to do this successfully, and on a regular basis, you could take this task to the next level. Start writing down the tasks you need to do for the week. The moment you get a new task, write it down. Allow your mind to process the work that needs to be done. It will also help you develop a sense of urgency much earlier than expected. When we leave our plans to our mind, we tend to relax and think that we have more time than we actually do. When you have your plans on paper, you have a realistic representation of how much time you actually do have. Eventually, this small step will lead to you having better organizational skills and it will also curb the overwhelming feeling you receive when you think of all the work that you need to do.

2. Set daily reminders for yourself.

Sometimes, writing down everything that you need to do might not be enough for you – especially if you are a forgetful person. This is why I would like to encourage you to consider setting reminders for yourself. Your phone would be the perfect thing to use to set these reminders. Every phone comes with a set of alarms that you can set according to your day, so that you don't forget the things that you need to do. If you are the type of person who is unable to stick to checking a diary or a scheduler, then add this task to support the first step. Try to set the reminders at least an hour before a task needs to be started. It will stop you from getting lost in the current task you are doing, and it will also mentally prepare you for what else needs to be done. This step will also help you deal with the overwhelming feeling you may get when you feel like you have too much work. It will also assist you with rousing the motivation that you need to get the job done. On a larger scale, this task will assist you with the struggles you may have with managing your time and keeping your schedule in order.

3. Make use of resources that will help you improve your skills deficit.

Fear of failure and a consciousness of lacking skills are two of several major root causes for procrastination. The best way to start small with tackling this issue is to compile a list of the areas in which you are struggling. Once you have managed to write this list down, you will be surprised to find that the skills you were worried about actually aren't as many as you may think they are. Our minds have a way of magnifying our problems. Once you have compiled this list, turn to the internet and start to search for basic ways to improve these skills. For example, if you are a slow typist, there are many free resources that you can use to improve this skill. Take it one day at a time, practice regularly, and your typing skills will be improved. When you are able to type faster, a number of projects that you used to dread won't be as daunting anymore. You won't fear failure as much when you have confidence in your abilities. The sight of continuous progress has a way of curbing the angst that one gets when they think of failure. Eventually, you won't put off tasks that require typing. The confidence that you will have in your typing skills will motivate you to get the job done without worry. This method isn't exclusive to typing skills. You can apply this approach to many skills. Identify the problem, find suitable, gradual ways to remedy them, and allow your confidence to motivate you. It is the small things, like gradually working on your lacking skills, which will contribute to large amounts of progress.

I should warn you now that if you do choose to "start small", there will come a time where you will feel frustrated about the progress you feel that you are not making. This is natural. When you are focused on making a change in your life, your drive will lead to moments of impatience – especially when it seems like nothing is happening. In times like this, you have to remind yourself that this is a process and it will take time for things to change. You don't need to beat yourself up for feeling impatient. There is nothing wrong with it. You are just determined to handle your life in a better way. Your impatience is justified. What you need to do, however, is make sure that your impatience doesn't lead you to making rash decisions. Impatience is known to compel a person to make decisions that end up setting them back several steps, instead of moving them forward.

Another thing that you will need to look out for is discouragement. It tends to slip in when you least expect it to. As I mentioned before, this process takes time. There are times where you will relapse and find yourself procrastinating all over again. Sometimes, you will feel fed up and you will want to quit. Procrastination isn't a small thing – especially when it has become a lifelong habit. People treat it like a trivial thing because of its seemingly harmless nature, but when you take a look at the root causes of many cases of stress and burnout you will find procrastination in the center of it all. Another reason why people who struggle with procrastination tend to become discouraged during their process of changing is because of the pressure they give themselves to do better. Procrastinators are seen as people who are irresponsible. They rarely receive any empathy or understanding. Most people tell them to get their act together. This adds to a procrastinator's guilt and it makes them want to rush the process of improving. If you find yourself feeling discouraged about the process, don't give up. It's normal to feel discouraged every now and then. You simply want to do better for yourself and you hope to do it as fast as possible. When you don't see your desired results, it's understandable as to why you would end up feeling discouraged. In those moments of discouragement, remind yourself that you are in the middle of a process and things will become better. Sometimes we need to remind ourselves of where we are headed in order to keep moving forward.

Chapter 5
Parkinson's Law

"Work expands so as to fill the time available for its completion."

– Cyril Parkinson

Cyril Parkinson coined this statement during his time working in the British Civil Service. His first-hand observations of bureaucracy and how it functions allowed him to come to the understanding of the relationship between time and a system's rate of productivity. Bureaucracy can be said to be a by-product of human culture. Parkinson observed that the systems within bureaucracy strove to fill time with working on tasks – regardless of their importance – in order to justify their existence to the public. In simpler terms, Parkinson noticed that human beings tended to elaborate the amount of work they had to do in order to fill time. Instead of striving to finish the given task within a short amount of time, Cyril noticed that members within the service resorted to stretching the tasks over a longer amount of time until the last minute. He also noticed that sense of urgency that would come over individuals when the deadline for the task was nearing.

Parkinson took to studying different institutions and individuals to determine whether this was a common practice among human beings. He discovered that it was. Human beings tend to stretch their work over a certain period of time, as opposed to trying to finish the task as soon as possible.

I'll use a scenario to explain this better:

If you are given two weeks to complete an assignment that can be completed in two hours, psychologically speaking, the task will appear to be more complicated than you initially thought it was. Your reaction will be to spend the next two weeks working on the task, instead of attempting to finish the task in two hours. You won't necessarily spend those two weeks attempting to work on the assignment – as you said you would. No. It's very likely that you will spend the majority of those two weeks deliberating over the assignment, feeling guilty for not doing it, and stressing about how complicated your mind has perceived the task to be. But when the two weeks are coming to an end, and the deadline for the assignment is close by, you suddenly find that you are able to handle the task and all the complexities that were preventing you from doing it in the first place. Nothing would have changed within those two weeks. The thought of the deadline being in view rouses a sense of urgency which leads you to working on the assignment. You become willing to finish the assignment at all costs – even if it means staying up all night in order to finish it.

This is all psychological. The task didn't become harder to accomplish on its own. That is how your mind chose to perceive it. The more you dwelled on the task, the more daunting it appeared to be. Because of this, you convinced yourself that you didn't need to try and tackle the assignment within two hours of receiving it. Instead, you felt that it would be best if you chose to use those two weeks to tackle the complexities that your mind conjured up. Most of the time, these mental perceptions and decisions are done unconsciously. The conscious decisions that you chose to make were actually inspired by subconscious influences.

This is what Parkinson was referring to when he coined the law, "work expands to fill the time available for its completion". It's not the work that changes; it is people who change the way the work appears to be.

One could view this as a form of mental sabotage because that is what it really is. If you look at this scenario from a logical point of view, you'll be exasperated by the fact that the person chose to use two weeks to complete a task that could have been completed in two hours. Surely one would want to get a task out of the way and use the excess time to do other things? In theory, yes, but the answer changes in a practical settings. Human beings have a way of sabotaging themselves – and they won't even know it. Procrastination is a form of unconscious self-sabotage. On the surface, you might think that you are doing yourself a favor by leaving the task for a more "favorable" time but that isn't what's actually happening. You've allowed yourself to become blind to the fact that there are better options at hand. Instead of seeing the benefits of finishing a task early, your mind chooses to see the necessity to prolong the task for as long as possible.

Here are a couple of other real-time scenarios where the average person has experienced Parkinson's Law:

- At the beginning of your semester, your class was assigned with a term paper. Your lecturer mentioned that the assignment would not take longer than two weeks to complete. She warned you that it would be best for you to plan out the assignment in order to avoid any last minute stress. Instead of choosing to handle the task in good time, you end up using the last 96 hours before the deadline to complete the assignment. You also end up submitting the project at 23:30 – half an hour before the assignment is due.

- Your mother informed you that she is coming to visit you in two months' time. You haven't cleaned your apartment in months and you know how tense your mother becomes when she finds herself in untidy conditions. Instead of clearing your apartment in advance, you end up spring cleaning your house the day before your mother is meant to be arriving. The large amount of work that needs to be done keeps you up all night and you manage to finish cleaning an hour before your mother arrives.

- You've decided to use the winter period to get fit and prepare your body for the summer and the beach vacation you planned with your college friends. Instead of choosing to work out immediately, you spend the winter period putting off your new fitness regime for the next day, week, or month. By the time spring arrives, and one month before the beach vacation, you go into overdrive and use the remaining four weeks to go on a crash diet and an intensive workout program.

People are often unable to describe why they can't work. The initial motivation they had disappears and is replaced by complacency. Whenever a person thinks of the task, they see the long amount of time they have to complete the task and they relax. "I've got all the time in the world. I'll start tomorrow." That tomorrow never comes until there is very little time left for the task to be completed. The way a person transforms from the complacent being to a hyperactive, proactive individual is almost surprising. There is something about people and managing to waste time.

During his time at the British Civil Service, Cyril Parkinson noticed that the larger a task became, the more its efficiency decreased. Simple tasks that could be completed within hours ended up being completed in weeks – and even months. As the time allocated to a task became less, suddenly, the task became easier to handle.

Hard Work vs Smart Work

Parkinson's Law confronts the problematic mentality that one needs to work hard instead of work smart. Smart work refers to working efficiently. Instead of sitting in a chair for hours and wiling time away by completing meaningless tasks, you use the available time to complete all the important tasks that need to be completed.

People tend to believe that the quality of your work is determined by the amount of time you spend to complete the work. This is why you find a lot of corporate institutions rewarding workers for the amount of hours they spend at work, instead of the hours they actually used to be productive. The truth is, you could spend long nights trying to work on a task but if you aren't making any reasonable progress then it means that you are wasting your time. It would be better for you to use two hours to complete a task properly, instead of using two weeks to waste time.

Unfortunately, you are not going to find many people who will encourage you to work smart. The world runs on the numerous hours that the labor force uses to "work". If you are going to implement Parkinson's Law in your life, which encourages you to work smart instead of "work hard", you're going to have to do it yourself.

You will need to implement your own version of limitations in order to work more efficiently. When you apply artificial limitations to the tasks that need to be done, your mind will be convinced that you don't have as much time as you anticipated and this will move you to work better.

This is a great way to work on the struggles you may have with time management. Improving your time management does not start with you purchasing a calendar and an alarm clock. These things may help on the surface but they will not deal with the root cause of the issue. Parkinson's Law has exposed that root issue – the mind. Parkinson observed that the reason why people stretch their tasks over a period of time is because of the way they have mentally perceived the difficulty of the task and the amount of time that they have to complete it. In order to change your mind's perception, you need to implement a few techniques that will change the way you view your work.

5. Time versus Results

Most people tend to set their targets according to a result-based target. For example, a person may set a target of ten thousand words to write in a day. Your mind will convince you that you have the whole day to do it, and you will end up procrastinating. If you want to work smart, let your target be time-based. Instead of wanting to write ten thousand words in a day, change the goal to wanting to finish writing a piece before midday. Your mind will become conscious of the new limitation and the way you perceive the task at hand. Instead of feeling relaxed about it, your mind will kick into work mode, thus propelling you to get the task done before the set time. This method works for exercise, errands, and any other tasks you often find yourself putting off. Instead of giving yourself the whole day to do them, focus on getting them done before a certain amount of time.

6. Remove that Charger

If you know that you are the type of person to waste time on the laptop before you get the job done, you could give this tactic a shot. Instead of giving yourself the whole day to finish a task that you need to do on your PC, unplug your charger and focus on finishing the task before your battery dies. If you don't trust yourself, you could ask someone you trust to keep your laptop charger while you work. That way, you won't cheat and attempt to charge your laptop halfway through completing the task. This is a great way to artificially restrict your time. Your mind will become focused on doing the necessary work at hand, instead of drifting off to distractions like social media, games, movies, etc.

7. **Get an accountability partner**

An accountability partner is someone who will help you overcome your procrastination by holding you accountable to the tasks that you have promised to do. Sometimes, it can be hard to be personally accountable. Accountability partners exist in order to help you improve your personal accountability. It becomes easier to stick to your promises when you know that there is someone watching out for you. Your accountability partner can also "punish" you if you fail to complete your tasks within the allocated time. Punishments could be in the form of fines, written tasks, public apologies, etc. The main goal at the end of the day is to get you to do your work on time.

8. Set a solid deadline.

This will be effective for any fitness or health-related tasks that you need to do. If you've been struggling with trying to stick to working out on your own, you could resort to finding a fitness program that could work for you. For example, you could choose to sign up for a four or eight-week fitness program that comprises of a number of goals that will help you remain. Eight weeks is your solid deadline – it cannot be changed. To make the program more exciting for yourself, set a target goal for the end of those eight weeks. "By the end of these eight weeks I want to be able to…" – fill in the rest of the sentence. Understand that you will not be able to achieve your dream body or dream weight in eight weeks, but the program will give you a big push in the right direction. A feasible goal could be "By the end of these eight weeks, I want to be able to do eighty pushups, straight." Use a journal to record your journey – it will also help you remain accountable. If you don't trust yourself, you can get an accountability partner to help you remain focused on sticking to the program.

9. Limit the tedious tasks.

Our daily lives include tedious tasks that tend to take up a lot of our time. The tedious nature of these tasks is what has us taking unnecessarily large amounts of time to complete them. Responding to emails is a prime example of a tedious task that tends to take up a lot of time. No one likes having to deal with a barrage of emails – especially first thing in the morning. A typical response to a full inbox of emails is to go through them as slowly as possible. The problem with this response is that it ends up affecting the rest of one's day. Instead of spending endless hours on your inbox, give yourself a time limit. Thirty minutes is an ideal amount of time to spend on emails. You could choose to check your emails every three hours for no more than thirty minutes. The rest of the time will be used to focus on making sure that you complete more important tasks.

These are a few of the best tactics you can use to tackle the mental block in your mind that aids your procrastination. Once again, you need to remember that it will take time for these tactics to yield long-lasting results. You also need to remember that this is all part of the process. There may be days where your attempts to curb the time you spend on checking emails will fail, and that's okay. Just keep working on it and eventually you'll be functioning like clockwork.

Parkinson's Law is not a complex method that you have to try and grasp as quickly as possible. It is simply provides you with a clearer view on the causes of procrastination and poor time management. The tactics that we have provided will help you combat the mental obstacles you experience, and increase your motivation to get the job done in good time. It is an all-round win situation for you.

After a few weeks have passed, you will find your time management skills improving. The progress that you see will encourage you to keep at it and eventually, you'll be making greater strides towards overcoming your challenges with procrastinating.

Chapter 6
The Law of Three

Pareto Principle

The Pareto Principle is also known as the **80/20 Rule.** The principle states that eight percent of the results come from twenty percent of the effort.

This principle was coined by an Italian economist from the 19th century – Vilfredo Pareto. He came to this realization after he observed that eighty percent of his country's wealth belonged to twenty percent of the country's population.

This theory isn't just limited to countries and their economies. The Pareto principle is evident in many facets of life. The **80/20** ratio is an estimation – it is not a fixed ratio. You could find instances where ninety-nine percent of the outcome is a result of one percent of the input.

The Pareto principle works against the belief that in order for a person to attain a large amount of success, they need to put in an equal amount of hard work. Hard work is a concept that has come to glorify hours and hours of laborious work, regardless of its efficacy. Many corporates are not concerned with whether a person is effective or not. People are only concerned with seeing their employees working. Employees are not encouraged to work smart. They are instructed work hard in order to gain the approval of their superiors. The problem is that the hard work concept drains people of their energy, and leaves little room for them to be innovative or efficient. When a person has to focus on "working as hard as possible" on a regular basis, it is inevitable that they will become tired. Procrastination can also be a result of fatigue. A person will become tired of the high demand that they experience on a daily basis. Instead of trying to reduce their workload, they'll simply resort to not doing anything.

If you choose to follow a "work as hard as possible" approach when it comes to your daily task, you will end up losing steam. You cannot channel a high level of work energy into several tasks at the same time. Something will have to give eventually. The Pareto Principle encourages you to use your time to focus on the more important tasks, instead of trying to give all of your energy to every task that is on your to-do list. For example, the amount of energy that you channel into filing an urgent report should not be the same amount of energy you use to check your emails. That is an example of misusing your time and focus.

The Pareto Principle can be explained in the following

illustration:

A man is transporting a group of animals on a ship when he encounters a raging storm. The following animals are on the boats: ten elephants, twelve lions, fifty monkeys, and one hundred lemmings. The man examines the animals and discovers that since there are more lemmings and monkeys, they should be thrown overboard in order to lighten the load.

The man's perception is quantity-based. It would have made more sense for him to get rid of their elephants. Elephants are the heaviest animals on the boat. The weight of fifty monkeys can barely reach the weight of two elephants. It would be far more effective for the man to throw the elephants overboard, in order to preserve the safety of everyone else on board.

In the same manner, a person should focus on the importance of the work that needs to be done, over the quantity of a workload.

These are a few more examples channeling your energy into the wrong tasks:

- Spending an hour going through 100 unimportant emails instead of using that time to work on a two-hour report.

- Spending one hour on the treadmill, instead of doing a series of strength workouts for the same period of time.

- Spending hours researching a task instead of distributing the time effectively so that you can research and write up the task at the same time.

The Pareto Principle tackles the belief that quantity is more important than quality. Using the same amount of energy on all of your tasks, regardless of their importance, is an example of possessing misplaced priorities.

This is how you can use the Pareto Principle to work efficiently and in good time, too:

1. **Write down all the tasks you need to do within a day**

    This is the best way to get started is to take note of all the things you need to accomplish within a day. Before you set out to do anything, take the time to write down all of your tasks – big and small. This will give you a clearer perspective on what needs to be accomplished. It also stops you from worrying or panicking. Getting things out of your mind and onto paper is good way to relieve stress. It stops you from over- or underestimating your workload and it will help you plan effectively. You should make sure that you don't take longer than fifteen minutes to make your to-do list. Anything longer and you are wasting time.

2. Identify the main goal

Peruse your list and rate every task according to its level of importance. There will be some tasks that will require more of your intention than others. The tasks that are more important are tasks with urgent deadlines, tasks that will bring in better results, etc. The less important tasks tend to be the ones that won't require a lot of time or energy. An example of a high-importance task is starting a term project, writing up a work report, analyzing data that is needed within the next hour, etc. After you have rated your tasks, determine your main goals. For example, you could aim to finish all your high-importance tasks before lunch. Your main goal could be to finish working out by a particular time. The main goal must cover the important tasks.

3. Cut out the dead weight

Dead weight are the tasks on your to-do list that do not require a high amount of energy or focus. Going through your emails, sorting out your filing cabinet, using long hours to exercise are a few examples of dead-weight tasks. These tasks should not require the same amount of energy and focus as the important tasks. Once you have established your main goal for the day or a period of time throughout your day, block out the unimportant tasks. This will stop you from becoming distracted. Focusing on dead-weight tasks, instead of the important ones, is a form of procrastination. In order to curb this habit, you need to remove those distractions from your mind until you have completed the important tasks.

4. Channel your focus into the important work

Now that you have managed to separate the important tasks from the unimportant tasks, you can use the time that you have set aside to focusing on getting the important work done. Since you haven't wasted energy on the dead-weight tasks, you will be able to focus better. Your list has helped you prioritize and this will allow you to work calmly and confidently. Once you have completed the important tasks, you will be free to handle the dead-weight tasks without any stress.

The Pareto Principle stops you from producing rushed work and it also saves you from becoming stressed about your workload. This method helps you see your tasks from an achievable point-of-view and it helps you use your time effectively.

Parkinson's Law and the Pomodoro Technique

This section of the chapter will focus on a key part of Parkinson's Law that can effectively help with procrastination – the Pomodoro Technique.

The Pomodoro technique is a method used to help improve a person's discipline when it comes to time management and getting started with the important work. Most of the time, people end up procrastinating because they are unable to get started with the task. Some drown in an overload of emails before they are able to tackle the more important work. Others struggle to put their shoes on and go out for the jog they've been meaning to complete for days. There are also those who become caught up in trying to develop their skills before applying for a new job.

The lack of motivation is also a major reason why people feel that they are unable to get started with the important work. Many people believe that they can only work when they are motivated or inspired. If that sense of determination is not present, neither is their productivity. Instead of trying to do the task, regardless of how they may be feeling, procrastinators spend their time focusing on less important tasks. They call this "waiting for inspiration". When asked about when the inspiration or motivation is expected to arrive, procrastinators will often shrug and say that they are not sure. This is common, but not exclusive to, people who work in the creative field.

The problem is that this "lack of motivation" belief is a major stumbling block with many people who have the potential to produce great work. This belief enables laziness and poor time management. It allows a person to be comfortable with their nonchalance towards not getting a task done on time. People are not meant to wait on inspiration. Contrary to what a lot of people may believe, inspiration is not an esoteric force that goes around visiting whomever it desires. Inspiration is generated from within. A person is capable of motivating themselves into doing the work that they need to do. They are not left helpless until the light bulb flashes. They are highly capable of turning on that light bulb for themselves.

The Pomodoro techniques is a method that assists a person with generating the motivation they require to finish the tasks that they need to complete. One of the reasons why a person may end up becoming discouraged by the amount of work that they have to do is because of how they are viewing it. A person may look at their workload, think that it is too much to handle, and put it off until they feel that they can handle it.

The Pomodoro technique, named after the Pomodoro kitchen timer, is based on the idea that taking frequent breaks allows the brain to focus better.

In its simplest form, the Pomodoro Technique involves splitting work into twenty-five minute blocks or chunks, with a three to five minute break in between. After four chunks have gone by, one should take a longer break. This longer break should be fifteen to thirty minutes. This method suggests that the regular breaks increase the brain's ability to process information, thus resulting in more efficient productivity.

The Pomodoro technique doesn't require a lot of tools. The best way to approach this technique is to go old school. Using a pen, a piece of paper, and a timing device, you will be able to keep track of your time effectively.

If you are more technologically-inclined, you could make use of a phone or desktop app.

Your chunks of time don't have to be twenty-five minutes. You should experiment with different time intervals in order to find what works for you. The reason why I would recommend that you use the more old-school approach when using this method is because it will prevent you from becoming distracted. Mobile phones are always buzzing with notifications. If you open your tracking application to check your progress, there is a high chance that you will end up becoming distracted by other things which will lead you to wasting the time in your set.

This is a step-by-step process on how to execute the technique yourself. Remember – simplicity is key.

1. **Choose a task that you would like to complete.**

    The task should be something you should be able to complete within one Pomodoro (twenty-five minutes). Start small with this technique. Once you've become accustomed to it, you can try working on completing longer task over more pomodori.

2. **Set your timer to twenty-five minutes.**

    If this is your first time trying out this method, then I suggest that you stick to the simplest time. You can use longer intervals once you've gained a grasp of the method.

3. **Work on the task until the timer rings.**

    The purpose of having a piece of paper by your side is to write down any distractions that may come to your mind. Once you have written them down, ignore them and focus on the task at hand. If you are interrupted by a phone call or anything else, write it down and postpone it until you are done with your task.

4. **Once you have completed a Pomodoro, tick it off or mark it with an x.**

   This is to help you keep a track of your progress and encourage you to carry on with the rest of the task. The sense of accomplishment that you will experience will serve as motivation for completing another set of twenty-five minutes.

5. **Take not of the number of times you were distracted during the twenty-five minutes.**

   This will help you identify the areas in which you need to improve.

6. **After completing a Pomodoro, remember to take a three to five minute break.**

   This will help you refresh and prepare for the next set of work.

7. **Take a fifteen to thirty minute break after every forth Pomodoro.**

   Grab something to eat, stretch your limbs, and check your emails and notifications during this period of time.

These are few reasons as to why the Pomodoro Technique works so well:

1. **It improves the way you focus.**

   The Pomodoro technique allows you to postpone all interruptions in order to focus on the work at hand. The use of regular breaks allows you to refresh so that you are able to work effectively when you have to return to your work. This method also prevents burn out because you are working in twenty-five minute intervals.

2. **It makes your work look more appealing.**

   The thought of sitting at your desk for six to eight hours can be very daunting. It's enough to make a person procrastinate until they feel ready to work. But when you are able to take your day, twenty-five minutes at a time, it makes your work look far more appealing. You become less intimidated and more motivated to get started.

Handling your work task by task is also much more pleasant that sitting down to simply "work". If you know that you are currently focusing on one task, instead of attempting to balance them all in your mind, it will be much easier for you to get started.

3. It assists you with working faster

The thought of a nearing deadline is enough to make a person up their work speed in order to get the job done. When you are working to the sound of a ticking timer, or you have a timer in view, it inspires you to give the task your all.

Taking notes of your work and your progress also gives you a clearer perspective on the areas in which you are excelling in, as opposed to the areas that need improvement. This technique prevents you from finding time to procrastinate.

4. It gives you a better understanding on how to work effectively

This technique doesn't just focus on making sure that you get the work done. Through recording your progress – and your distractions – this method allows you to analyze the way you perform your work. By taking note of your performance, you are able to adjust the way you work accordingly. By manipulating the way you work, you are ultimately improving the way you get the job done, which will improve the quality of the work that you are producing.

These are a few things you need to be wary of when it comes to the Pomodoro technique:

- **It might not sync with your style of work**

    The Pomodoro technique is not the time management method of all time management methods. There is no one hundred percent guarantee that this method will work for you. But this shouldn't stop you from giving it a shot. This approach could either help you curb your procrastination and allow you to work better, or it may leave you feeling as if you are restricted. Either way, it would be best for you to try it out so that you can see if it works for you or not.

- **It does not accommodate half-hearted attempts.**

    When it comes to the Pomodoro technique, it's all or nothing. If you are interrupted during a pomodoro and you have to use the rest of the twenty-five minutes to handle that interruption, you are not allowed to mark that interval as successful. You have to start again.

In order to avoid wasting time, you have to plan your day and week in advance to ensure that nothing interferes with your pomodoros. You can also shorten the length of time in your pomodoros if that will work for you. The main goal is to finish all your pomodoros successfully in a day.

- **It is not for every type of work**

    Some people might not appreciate the fact that you have to use a timer in order to get your work done. What works for you might not work for someone else. This method is also highly dependent on your profession. If you work in a high-risk job, this method might not work well for you.

    But you can apply it to areas outside of work. The Pomodoro Technique can work for fitness, cleaning, running errands, paying your taxes, etc.

    If you are using it in an office, it would be advisable that you purchase headphones or find a quieter alarm so that you don't frustrate the people around you. Experiment with different alarms until you are able to find something that works for you.

When it comes to the Pomodoro Technique, you also need to make sure that you remain patient – this method may require a few days before you notice any major changes in your productivity. Always stick to your timer, don't try to cheat the process and make sure that you prioritize your tasks. Remember, the point of this technique is to help you manage your time efficiently in order to get the right work done.

Newton's First Law of Motion

This law is also known as the *Law of Inertia*.

The law states:

"Everybody remains in a state of constant velocity unless acted upon by an external unbalanced force"

In simpler terms: Whatever is at rest will remain at rest and whatever is in motion will continue to be in motion.

From a productivity perspective, it can be explained like this:

When a person is at rest – i.e. procrastinating – they will remain in this state of procrastination until they decide to change it (which would be the entrance of the aforementioned "external unbalanced force".

If you choose to put off your work, and relax for the meanwhile, nothing is going to stop you from relaxing until you decide to make a change. Your procrastination will remain as perpetual because of your lack of desire to become active. The Law of Inertia gives an accurate description on what occurs when a person chooses to procrastinate. Their state remains as perpetual.

This is how a person will continue to find things to distract them from the main task at hand until they finally decide to become productive.

In order to overcome procrastination, you need to find a way to start that task as fast as possible.

This correlates with the other part of the Law of Inertia: whatever is in motion will remain in motion.

Once you have managed to start working, you will remain motivated to keep on working until you get the job done. A procrastinator's biggest challenge is getting started with that work. Many people who procrastinate experience a big mental block when it comes to trying to get started with a task.

When someone is given a task to complete, they are presented with two choices – get started with the work or become distracted. There is a very short-time frame for this decision to be made. If a person could just overcome that mental block that stops them from working immediately, they would be able to deal with their procrastination. Procrastination comes into full swing when a person entertains it. Once they have entered that state, it is very hard to come out of it.

The only way to overcome this mental block is to just get started with the work. It may sound like an oversimplified instruction but it's a fact. In order to beat procrastination, you have to get into the motion of working as soon as possible.

This needs to be done within two minutes of receiving a task, otherwise you will be leaving room for distractions to take away your focus.

Once you have managed to achieve that state of work, you'll find yourself completing that task in good time. The sense of accomplishment that you will experience will motivate you to get started with another task as soon as possible.

Chapter 7
Rewards

Overcoming a habit and replacing it with a better one is no small feat. Habits are not easy to kick – especially when you have accommodated them for most of your life. People tend to make it seem like it's a walk in the park but this could not be any further from the truth. It takes patience, resolve, and lots of self-forgiveness to overcome habits that hinder one from realizing their full potential. We have already established the deep-rooted challenges that one faces when they are trying to deal with their habit of procrastination. It's not just about not knowing how to handle your time.

Overcoming procrastination may require you to do an internal reflection that will unearth secrets and feelings you had chosen to hide. Dealing with triggers like the fear of failure and a lack of confidence in one's skills can be an emotionally exhausting task. Do not allow anyone to make kicking procrastination sound like it requires little effort. The process forces a person to deal with their shortcomings in order to become a better person. No one likes to deal with their flaws. Very few people appreciate focusing on the areas in which they are lacking. Even though it may be for the greater good, it doesn't stop the process from being emotionally taxing.

This is why it would be a great idea for you to incorporate a rewards system into your journey. Rewards are your way of telling yourself that you are doing a great job. The journey to overcoming a habit like procrastination is often seen as a quiet, and sometimes lonely, journey. People don't see procrastination as a difficult thing to overcome. This is why procrastinators receive little to no support or sympathy. You have to be your biggest fan if you intend on making progress in your personal development.

Rewarding yourself will remind your mind that you are making progress. It will help you deal with the difficult days and it will boost your motivation on the good days. The journey to overcoming procrastination consists of many ups and downs. A reward system will help you maintain consistent progress, regardless of anything that comes your way.

Moments that are worth rewarding are dependent on you. There is no fixed way on how you should reward yourself. If you would like to reward yourself after completing a day of achieving goals, then do so. If you would like to reward yourself at the end of the month, that can work too. The thing that matters the most is that you acknowledge the fact that you are gaining ground on making your goals become a reality.

Here are a few ways in which you can reward yourself

for a job well done:

- **It boosts and maintains your motivation.**

    Rewards are a great way of boosting your motivation when you have a lot of work to get through. Rewarding yourself with breaks throughout your day will help you maintain your focus whilst you are working. A reward could come on the form of ten minute breaks to do whatever you want to do before getting back to work. The Pomodoro Technique has incorporated this form of self-rewarding in their method.

    Getting through a whole day can be very challenging for anyone. When you reward yourself, you are reminding yourself that you are doing your best and that is what counts. Motivation plays a key part in getting the job done.

    Another example could be rewarding yourself with a healthy snack after managing to complete a successful session at the gym. The sense of accomplishment, coupled with the reward, will motivate you to keep up with your fitness program.

    If you manage to complete fifty percent of the spring cleaning job in your house, you could take a break to reward yourself with a treat like ice-cream, or an hour to watch a show of your choice. Acknowledging that you've managed to do half the job will motivate you to complete it once your job done. Once you see that you are able to complete a task without procrastinating, it will be easier for you to become motivated the next time you have to spring clean your house.

Motivation boosters are great for a person's productivity. It helps them believe that they are well-equipped to finish a task successfully.

- **It makes you feel good.**

    The sense of accomplishment that comes with completing a task – especially a task that required a lot of energy – is indescribable. Not only does rewarding yourself motivate you, it makes you feel good about yourself. Procrastinators often beat themselves up about the fact that they are unable to manage their time properly in order to get a job done on time. They liken themselves to failures. When you manage to go against the urge to procrastinate and you successfully complete a goal, rewarding yourself will give you the validation you need to believe that you are capable of completing work on time.

Confidence is everything. A person cannot be successful without confidence. Rewarding yourself can help you stir up the confidence you need to continually work at overcoming your habit of procrastinating.

The reward does not need to be an over-the-top reward in order for you to feel good about yourself. As long as it is something meaningful, it will help boost the way you feel about yourself. People find it easier to criticize themselves. Do the opposite of this.

If you manage to accomplish a long-term goal, your reward could be something that boosts your wellbeing – a trip to the spa or a wellness center for example. Rewarding yourself with a gift like a book could boost your mental wellbeing. Let your rewards be things that are able to boost your mind and your body.

The sense of fulfillment that you will get from rewarding yourself for a job well done will work wonders for your self-confidence and your self-worth. People who hold themselves in high regard are more likely to succeed in life. Make sure that you are one of those people.

- **It validates your progress.**

    Rewards remind you of the progress that you have been making. When you set high expectations for yourself, it is very easy for you to overlook the moments of progress you make in a day or a week. A procrastinator's ultimate goal is to stop procrastinating. That is a goal that will be achieved over a long period of time through different means and methods. If a person decides that they are going to wait for that goal to be achieved before they reward themselves, they may end up becoming discouraged along the way.

    Overcoming procrastination happens in moments. With every task that is completed in good time, and every distraction resisted, a person comes one step closer to overcoming their struggle with procrastination. The process of overcoming procrastination is made up of small moments of victory. If a person fails to acknowledge the progress they make on a daily basis, they will become discouraged. In their discouragement, they will believe that they aren't making any significant progress.

    This is why it is important for you to track your progress. It gives you a clearer understanding of your progress over a period of time. Tracking your progress also assists with keeping you motivated while you are in the middle of completing a number of tasks.

Rewards are your way of telling yourself that you have taken note of your progress and you approve of it. Rewarding yourself for the progress that you have made alerts your mind to the fact that what you are doing is good and you should continue to do it.

- **It encourages you to put in more effort.**

    Rewarding yourself doesn't just encourage you to finish the tasks at hand. They motivate you to put in more effort to become a better worker, athlete, etc. When you become aware of the good work that you are doing, it will motivate you to do more. Everyone loves being rewarded for their good work. In order to maintain that gratification, your mind will instruct you to put in more effort.

    You will be encouraged to set more goals for yourself. Once you have noticed that you are able to achieve the goals you set for yourself, you will want to achieve more. If you doubted yourself before, after rewarding yourself for your progress your doubts will dwindle. Confidence will replace your reservations and you will feel as if you can achieve anything. That is the right mindset to have when it comes to overcoming a habit.

The majority of this battle is in the mind. Rewarding yourself if a form of positive reinforcement that will motivate you to increase the quality of your performance. As the quality of your work performance improves, so will the quality of the work you produce. Not only will you be pleased with yourself. You will be making your clients, colleagues, peers, and loved ones much happier. That, in itself, is a reward worth achieving.

Chapter 8
Working with Yourself

You cannot afford to see yourself as the enemy. That is one of the fastest ways to counter any form of progress you may have been able to make. If anything, working against yourself will hinder you from making any considerable progress. Working against yourself to self-loathing which will create more problems for yourself. You should not allow your mistakes to define you. Procrastination does not define who you are. Simply view it as a habit that needs to be overcome.

The way you treat yourself will directly influence the progress that you aspire to make. People tend to underestimate the effect their beliefs and attitudes will have on themselves. We always focus on how our actions and words will affect other people, but we rarely take time to consider how they might make us feel or act. The most important view in a person's life is their perception of themselves. How you perceive yourself will affect the way you function in life. If you choose to view yourself from a resentful point-of-view, you are only working against yourself.

People tend to believe that when it comes changing something about your life, you have to treat yourself as the enemy. Motivators tend to encourage people to view themselves as the problem that needs to be solved. This may sound good to hear, but it doesn't work well for your personal development. Personal development is about aiming to make yourself *better*, not viewing yourself as a problem that needs to be fixed. There are a lot of negative connotations that are associated with viewing yourself as a problem to be fixed. It only serves as a means to knock your confidence.

You cannot afford to see yourself as the enemy. The guilt you experience from procrastinating is more than enough negativity that you can afford to accommodate in your life.

Overcoming procrastination is a form of personal development. Self-confidence is a major part of the process to develop yourself. You cannot make yourself a better person if you are doing it out of self-loathing. Viewing yourself as the enemy is a standard example of self-loathing. Self-confidence will help you make the leaps and bounds that you need to make in order to achieve progress in your life.

Procrastination has a way of making a person feel lowly about themselves. No one likes to let people down. Very few people enjoy being unable to stick to a schedule. These things have the ability to make a person feel useless. You need to be able to pick yourself up when no one else is around you.

Three of the most common ways of working against yourself are "tough love", a defeatist attitude, and comparing yourself to other people.

- **"Tough Love"**

    Some people tend to believe that they need to be hard on themselves in order to make a change in their lives. Most procrastinators are often encourage to be strict with themselves when it comes to trying to overcome their habit. They are encouraged to incorporate different forms of punishment for the times that they fail to fulfill a target that they set for themselves. They are also encouraged to use harsher words on themselves in order to help them overcome their tendency to procrastinate. People tend to believe that true discipline comes in the form of harsh words, a hard attitude, and making no room for mistakes. While this may sound good on paper, it rarely works in practice. Treating yourself harshly will only serve as a counterproductive action. The last thing you need is more pressure. "Tough love" will only cause you to pressure yourself more than you should be. That pressure may serve as a trigger, and cause you to feel overwhelmed or unconfident about your ability to finish the task at hand. This could lead to you deciding to put off the task – which is something you've been doing all along. When you fail to do the task in good time, you will only make things worse by being harsh on yourself.

I would not recommend this method to anyone. In order to make a change from a habit that was negatively affecting your life, you need to make room for mistakes. You need to give yourself the benefit of the doubt. You do *not* need to use negative reinforcement as a means of trying to get yourself to do the work.

The problem with negative reinforcement is the fact that while it may appear to be working, in the initial stages, it will only remain like that for a short period of time. At some point, your mind will become tired of the tension caused and it will revert to your former way of functioning.

Using "tough love" is an easy way for you to lose confidence in yourself. There is a fine line between holding yourself to a higher standard, and simply coming down on yourself like a ton of bricks. Only one of these options will help you – and it is not the latter option. To be disciplined does not mean that you need to be harsh on yourself.

- **A defeatist attitude**

    You're not going to make much progress is you

are already viewing the task as impossible to overcome. Being defeatist means that you have already given up before trying. This happens when you view your state as impossible to come. Serial procrastinators tend to feel as if they are unable to overcome their state because they are too far gone. If you choose to move forward with a mentality like that, you will not make any notable progress.

Having a defeatist attitude means that you are already setting yourself up for failure. You are expecting the failure to happen; to you, it is inevitable. On the day you fail to fulfil one of your goals, you simply shrug your shoulders and say that you saw it coming.

No one and nothing will ever be achieved by someone who choose to see themselves as a hopeless case. If anything, a defeatist attitude will lead you to procrastinating even more. This is a clear form of sabotage and if you are struggling with it, then you need to work towards getting rid of this attitude. The last thing you want or need is to be your biggest enemy. If you don't believe that you are capable of overcoming your procrastination, then that is what you will end up seeing.

In order to overcome this defeatist mentality, you need to be able to counter it with as many means of motivation as possible. The best way to get rid of an old mentality is to gradually replace it with a new one.

Instead of focusing on how hard it will be to stop procrastinating, focus on how great you will feel after making progress. Let that feeling be the motivation that keeps you going. If anyone around you is enabling your defeatist mentality, then you need to block those people out. You cannot afford to accommodate any skepticism during this time of your life.

Force your mind to focus on the positive side of your journey. You have chosen to make your life better – that is something to congratulate yourself about. Not everyone is willing to make the decision that you have made for your life. View yourself as a different person. Identify the good in yourself and magnify those thoughts in your mind. Instead of viewing yourself as a failure, view yourself as the kind of person who is able to turn around a situation. Adopt a winning mentality to counter any forms of defeatism that you may have allowed into your life.

- **Comparing yourself to other people**

Another reason why people try to improve themselves is so that they can become like the people around them. There is nothing wrong with being inspired by the people in your life. However, this becomes a problem when you constantly compare yourselves to them. Talking down on yourself and wishing that you were like someone else is a very fast way to tearing down any confidence you may have had in yourself. You need to understand that just because some people may appear to have a seemingly better grip on their lives, it doesn't make you any less of a person. You are not defined by other people's lives. Focus on your journey and on your progress. That is what matters the most. There will come a point where you will be able to overcome your shortcomings and you will be a more efficient worker because of it.

One of the best things you can do for yourself is to become your biggest fan. There is only so much that the people around you can do for you as you strive to overcome a habit that has held you down for so long. There are times where people will not be able to reach you and you'll have to pick yourself up on your own. There will also be times where you'll feel as if you are all alone on your journey towards becoming a better person. As I mentioned earlier in this book, people tend to view procrastinators as people who are unable to get a grip of their lives. This one thing can stop anyone from pushing on in their journey of overcoming. But it doesn't have to stop you. When you choose to be your biggest fan, you allow yourself to base your journey on yourself and not on the thoughts or opinions of other people.

The problem with relying on the praises of other people is that your progress will be affected when they do not give you the positive reinforcement that you need. Your journey to becoming a better person, and overcoming procrastination, needs to be rooted in the fact that you want to do it for yourself. You need to be willing to encourage and affirm yourself when the going gets tough. You need to be the first one to congratulate yourself when you find that you've made a significant amount of progress.

Your attitude towards yourself will play a major role in your journey to overcoming procrastination. If you know that you do not appreciate yourself the way you should, then you need to change that as soon as possible. There is a form of appreciation that you can only give yourself – no one else can do it for you.

One of the best ways to change the way you view yourself – and cheer yourself on - is through daily affirmations. Daily affirmations are one of the best ways to remind yourself of your self-worth. They serve as reminders of who you are, the greatness you possess, and the journey that is ahead of you. Sometimes, the journey will become tough and finding the strength to carry on will be close to impossible. Daily affirmations are one of the best ways to help you clear your mind and find the motivation that you need in order to carry on with your personal journey.

You are going to have to remind yourself of this statement over and over again: Be easy on yourself.

While seeking to overcome this habit, that has managed affect your daily life, it can become very easy to become critical of yourself when you aren't seeing any progress.

If you continue to be critical of and harsh towards yourself, all of the effort you've put into dealing your procrastination will go to waste.

Understand this: You have been dealing with your procrastination for a long period of time – months, years, your whole life – it will take time before you start seeing the progress you want to see.

You will have days that are good and it will feel like you are well on your way to remaining on top of your challenges; but you will also have days that won't be as good. You will have days where it will feel like all of your efforts are useless and you will question why you bothered trying.

You will experience times where it will feel like your procrastination is becoming worse. In those times, you need to remind yourself that you are on a journey and this journey is going to have ups and downs but it does not mean that you aren't moving forward. You need to keep in mind that every step you take to dealing with your habit of procrastinating, is another step in the direction of progress – even when it does not feel like it.

The purpose of this books is to offer you practical steps that are most successful when they are done over a long period of time. That is the thing about life – the most worthwhile things are built over long periods of time. There is no quick-fix method for dealing with procrastination.

Your desire to deal with your procrastination may build up a need for it to happen quickly; don't feel guilty about this. Take it easy on yourself. The main thing you need to focus on is not sabotaging your progress by being hard on yourself; you'll only make yourself feel worse and you might trigger a panic attack or another dark spell.

You also need to make allowances for yourself. Acknowledge that mistakes are natural – they are simply a part of life. Maintain the mindset that it will take you a number of attempts before you are able to get something right – and this does not mean that there is anything wrong with you as a person. Your relationship with yourself is a key component of dealing with your mental health and the challenges that you encounter on a daily basis.

The state of your relationship with yourself is often one

of the underlying triggers for procrastination. Insecurity and self-deprecation are common triggers in individuals who struggle with procrastination – it often stems from feeling frustrated with your inability to get a grip of your habit. The attitudes that you receive from other people can also play a major role in your frustration.

These are thoughts and belief one holds for years. Dealing with procrastination is similar to losing weight – it may take longer to get rid of it, but it sure will be worth it.

A couple of the methods that you found in this book have a lot to do with how you see yourself and how you will interact with your mind. Your mind plays a very important part in how you handle your tasks and how you view yourself as a person.

Your mind will also play a vital role in changing your life. Both of these things are hinged on your perception of yourself and your reaction to your progress. Knowing that you play a major role in your recovery should not make you feel like you are under pressure to produce results in the form of progress.

You should not allow any form of pressure to make you rush the process. This is a process that will take time. I will continue to say this until you believe it.

When you fail to keep to a deadline, or you find yourself doing a large amount of work late at night - don't beat yourself up about it; don't even try to fight it. Sometimes fighting the feelings will make you feel worse.

Don't feel guilty because it happened; you are recovering, moments like this will happen. Whatever you do, do not allow your mind to convince you that you are a failure because of a couple of bad days – because that's exactly what those low moments are, a couple of bad days that will pass. If you let your mind get the better of you, you will end up be feeding the very thing that is trying to hold you down.

I've developed a mantra you can repeat on the days you're experiencing a serious bout of discouragement.

"This is a process but regardless of what is happening I am still making progress – and that is what matters the most. It doesn't matter if I cannot see it or if I cannot feel it, I know that I am still making progress. I refuse to allow this procrastination to get the better of me. I am moving forward. I am getting better. I am making progress every single day."

I believe in the power of repetition and the power of positive speaking; they change one's outlook on life – one statement at a time. They give hope. In order for this journey to be fruitful, you need to be willing to try everything suggested – that is how you will find what will work for you. But, most importantly, you need to have hope; that is what will keep you going – especially when you feel like quitting.

These steps may sound like they are trivial to you if you've never understood the importance of cheering yourself on. But if you ask a number of successful people, they will tell you the exact same thing. You cannot make any substantial progress, on your own, if you are constantly working against yourself. When you get to a point of resenting yourself because of the mistakes you've made, your actions will be counterproductive. Instead of trying to work on freeing yourself from procrastination, you will spend that time listing reasons as to why you can't get anything write. When you work against yourself, you diminish all forms of self-confidence.

Self-confidence is an integral part of personal development. If you fail to see that, you are setting yourself up for failure. Failure will only worsen your belief in yourself and you'll find yourself in the middle of a damaging cycle. You will end up feeling as if you are incapable of achieving anything.

Self-confidence is required in order to make any notable progress in your life. If you aspire to be the type of person who can get a grasp on the way the work, and you desire to stop letting people done, then you need to be in support yourself.

Conclusion

I hope that you will be able to see this process through. My wish is for you to be able to work through the root causes that enable your procrastination. As you manage to deal with these roots, you will find it easier to handle tasks that you used to see as daunting. It will take time but it will happen. The important thing that you need to focus on is constantly reminding yourself that this is a process. Remind yourself as many times as you need to. Your mind and other external influences will try to make you feel as if your actions are not valid. Refer to the notes that you have taken to note your progress and use them to remind you of the strides that you have managed to make during this progress.

Procrastination may be a difficult habit to overcome but it is not impossible. If you pay attention to everything that you have read, you will find practical steps that will work for you and the challenges that you may be facing. Do not rush yourself with this process. When you mount unnecessary pressure on yourself, you are only setting yourself up for failure.

Affirm yourself every day and remind yourself that your personal development is possible. Challenges exist so that we can overcome them. There is nothing too big for you to overcome and I would like you to remind yourself of this on the days you feel as if you aren't making any progress.

There will be days where you will be able to get the job done without a hitch. But there will be days where those overwhelming feelings and fears will try to get the better of you. Allow yourself to make mistakes. It's part of the process.

Get up the next day and treat it like a fresh start. Write down your to-do list and do the work that matters.

You'll get the hang of it eventually.

"Just as we develop our physical muscles through overcoming opposition - such as lifting weights - we develop our character muscles by overcoming challenges and adversity."

Stephen Covey

Made in the USA
Columbia, SC
28 January 2018